Pearson Edexcel GCSE (9-1)

History

Weimar and Nazi Germany, 1918–1939

Series Editor: Angela Leonard   Author: John Child   Dan Nuttall

Published by Pearson Education Limited, 80 Strand, London, WC2R 0RL.

www.pearsonschoolsandfecolleges.co.uk

Copies of official specifications for all Edexcel qualifications may be found on the website: www.edexcel.com

Text © Pearson Education Limited 2018

Series editor: Angela Leonard
Designed by Colin Tilley Loughrey, Pearson Education Limited
Typeset by QBS Learning
Original illustrations © Pearson Education Limited
Illustrated by KJA Artists Illustration Agency, Phoenix Photosetting, Chatham, Kent and QBS Learning.

Cover design by Colin Tilley Loughrey
Cover photo © Front: Bridgeman Art Library Ltd: Private Collection

The rights of John Child and Dan Nuttall to be identified as authors of this work have been asserted by him in accordance with the Copyright, Designs and Patents Act 1988.

First published 2018

21 20
10 9 8 7 6 5 4

British Library Cataloguing in Publication Data
A catalogue record for this book is available from the British Library.
ISBN 978 1 292 25833 1

Printed in Great Britain by Ashford Colour Press Ltd

A note from the publisher
1. While the publishers have made every attempt to ensure that advice on the qualification and its assessment is accurate, the official specification and associated assessment guidance materials are the only authoritative source of information and should always be referred to for definitive guidance.

Pearson examiners have not contributed to any sections in this resource relevant to examination papers for which they have responsibility.

2. Pearson has robust editorial processes, including answer and fact checks, to ensure the accuracy of the content in this publication, and every effort is made to ensure this publication is free of errors. We are, however, only human, and occasionally errors do occur. Pearson is not liable for any misunderstandings that arise as a result of errors in this publication, but it is our priority to ensure that the content is accurate. If you spot an error, please do contact us at resourcescorrections@pearson.com so we can make sure it is corrected.

Websites
Pearson Education Limited is not responsible for the content of any external internet sites. It is essential for tutors to preview each website before using it in class so as to ensure that the URL is still accurate, relevant and appropriate. We suggest that tutors bookmark useful websites and consider enabling students to access them through the school/college intranet.

Contents

How to use this book

What's covered?

This book covers the Modern Depth study on Weimar and Nazi Germany, 1918–39. This unit makes up 30% of your GCSE course, and will be examined in Paper 2.

Modern depth studies cover a short period of time, and require you to know about a society or historical situation in detail. You need to understand different aspects within this period, such as social, economic, political, cultural and military, and how they interact with each other. This book also explains the different types of exam questions you will need to answer, and includes advice and example answers to help you improve.

Features

As well as a clear, detailed explanation of the key knowledge you will need, you will also find a number of features in the book:

Key terms

Where you see a word followed by an asterisk, like this: Allies*, you will be able to find a Key Terms box on that page that explains what the word means.

> **Key term**
>
> **Allies***
>
> The main Allies were Britain, France and the USA (Russia had pulled out of the war in 1917).

Activities

Every few pages, you'll find a box containing some activities designed to help check and embed knowledge and get you to really think about what you've studied. The activities start simple, but might get more challenging as you work through them.

Summaries and Checkpoints

At the end of each chunk of learning, the main points are summarised in a series of bullet points – great for embedding the core knowledge, and handy for revision.

Checkpoints help you to check and reflect on your learning. The Strengthen section helps you to consolidate knowledge and understanding, and check that you've grasped the basic ideas and skills. The Challenge questions push you to go beyond just understanding the information, and into evaluation and analysis of what you've studied.

Sources and Interpretations

This book contains numerous contemporary pictorial and text sources that show what people from the period, said, thought or created.

The book also includes extracts from the work of historians, showing how experts have interpreted the events you've been studying.

You will need to be comfortable examining both sources AND interpretations to answer questions in your Paper 3 exam.

> **Source A**
>
> A German poster from 1931. It advertises a NSDAP rally and shows a German figure in handcuffs labelled 'Versailles'.

> **Interpretation 1**
>
> From *The Coming of the Third Reich* by Richard J. Evans, published in 2004.
>
> No one was prepared for the peace terms... All of this was greeted with incredulous horror by the majority of Germans. The sense of outrage and disbelief... was almost universal. Germany's international strength and prestige had been on an upward course since unification in 1871... now, suddenly, Germany had been brutally expelled from the ranks of the Great Powers and covered in what they considered to be undeserved shame. Versailles was condemned as a dictated peace, unilaterally imposed without the possibility of negotiation.

Extend your knowledge

These features contain useful additional information that adds depth to your knowledge, and to your answers. The information is closely related to the key issues in the unit, and questions are sometimes included, helping you to link the new details to the main content.

> **Extend your knowledge**
>
> **Changing people's behaviour**
> Governments that want to change people's behaviour can't always do it by force. For example, the Nazis could not force women to have more children – but they could influence people's behaviour by changing the law.
>
> For example, as well as receiving marriage loans, women could also get monthly payments from the government to help with the cost of bringing up children.

Exam-style questions and tips

The book also includes extra exam-style questions you can use to practise. These appear in the chapters and are accompanied by a tip to help you get started on an answer.

Exam-style question, Section B

Study Source B (page 28) and Source F (page 31).

How useful are Source B and Source F for an enquiry into the recovery of the Weimar Republic between 1923 and 1929?

Explain your answer, using Source B, Source F and your knowledge of the historical context.   **8 marks**

Exam tip

A good answer will consider:

- how useful the information in each source is for this particular enquiry
- how the provenance (i.e. the type of source, its origin, author or purpose) of each source affects how useful it is
- how knowledge of history at that time affects a judgement of how useful each source is (note that one of the sources was created in 1923, when the situation was very bad, whereas the other was made in 1929, when things had improved slightly).

Recap pages

At the end of each chapter, you'll find a page designed to help you to consolidate and reflect on the chapter as a whole. Each recap page includes a recall quiz, ideal for quickly checking your knowledge or for revision. Recap pages also include activities designed to help you summarise and analyse what you've learned, and also reflect on how each chapter links to other parts of the unit.

THINKING HISTORICALLY

These activities are designed to help you develop a better understanding of how history is constructed, and are focused on the key areas of Evidence, Interpretations, Cause & Consequence and Change & Continuity. In the Modern Depth Study, you will come across activities on Cause & Consequence, Evidence and Interpretations as these are key areas of focus for this unit.

The Thinking Historically approach has been developed in conjunction with Dr Arthur Chapman and the Institute of Education, UCL. It is based on research into the misconceptions that can hold students back in history.

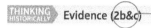 **Evidence (2b&c)** ⎯⎯⎯ conceptual map reference

The Thinking Historically conceptual map can be found at: www.pearsonschools.co.uk/thinkinghistoricallygcse

WRITING HISTORICALLY

At the end of most chapters is a spread dedicated to helping you improve your writing skills. These include simple techniques you can use in your writing to make your answers clearer, more precise and better focused on the question you're answering.

The Writing Historically approach is based on the *Grammar for Writing* pedagogy developed by a team at the University of Exeter and popular in many English departments. Each spread uses examples from the preceding chapter, so it's relevant to what you've just been studying.

Preparing for your exams

At the back of the book, you'll find a special section dedicated to explaining and exemplifying the new Edexcel GCSE History exams. Advice on the demands of this paper, written by Angela Leonard, helps you prepare for and approach the exam with confidence. Each question type is explained through annotated sample answers at two levels, showing clearly how answers can be improved.

Pearson Progression Scale: This icon indicates the Step that a sample answer has been graded at on the Pearson Progression Scale.

This book is also available as an online ActiveBook, which can be licensed for your whole institution.

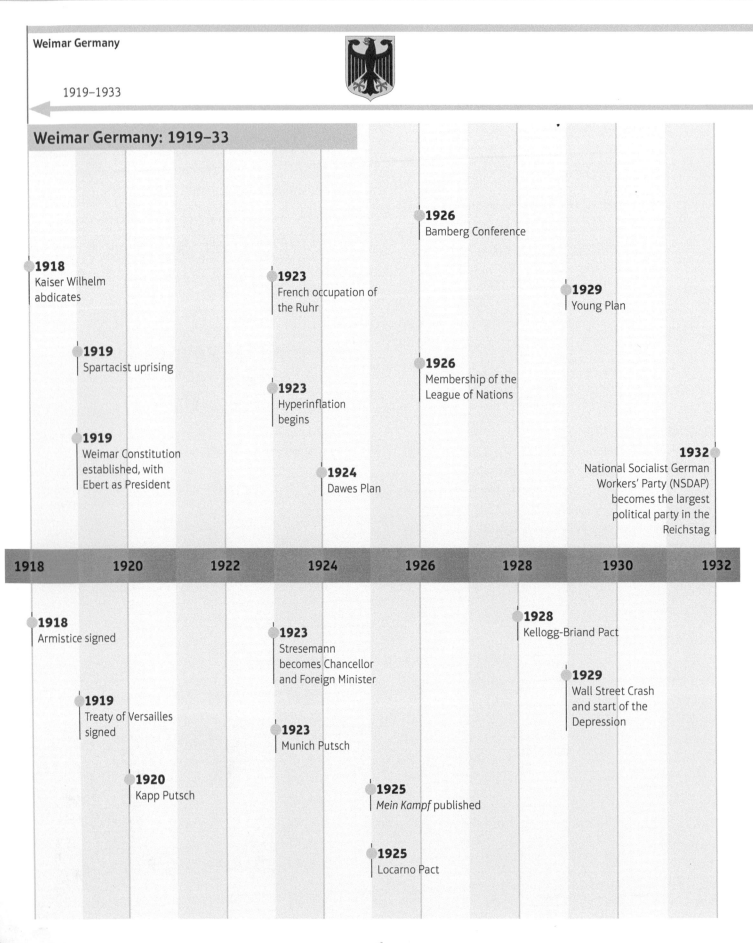

Weimar Germany

1919–1933

Weimar Germany: 1919–33

1926
Bamberg Conference

1918
Kaiser Wilhelm
abdicates

1923
French occupation of
the Ruhr

1929
Young Plan

1919
Spartacist uprising

1926
Membership of the
League of Nations

1923
Hyperinflation
begins

1919
Weimar Constitution
established, with
Ebert as President

1924
Dawes Plan

1932
National Socialist German
Workers' Party (NSDAP)
becomes the largest
political party in the
Reichstag

1918	1920	1922	1924	1926	1928	1930	1932

1918
Armistice signed

1923
Stresemann
becomes Chancellor
and Foreign Minister

1928
Kellogg-Briand Pact

1919
Treaty of Versailles
signed

1923
Munich Putsch

1929
Wall Street Crash
and start of the
Depression

1920
Kapp Putsch

1925
Mein Kampf published

1925
Locarno Pact

Nazi Germany

1933–1939

Nazi Germany: 1933–1945

1933
Hitler appointed as
Chancellor

1933
Reichstag Fire

1935
Nuremberg Laws
passed

1933
Enabling Law passed

1938
Kristallnacht
(Night of
Broken Glass)

1934
Night of the Long
Knives

| 1933 | 1934 | 1935 | 1936 | 1937 | 1938 |

1933
People asked to
boycott Jewish shops

1936
Berlin Olympics

1933
Gestapo (secret
police) established

1933
Concordat with
Catholic Church

1934
Death of Hindenburg
and Hitler becomes
Führer

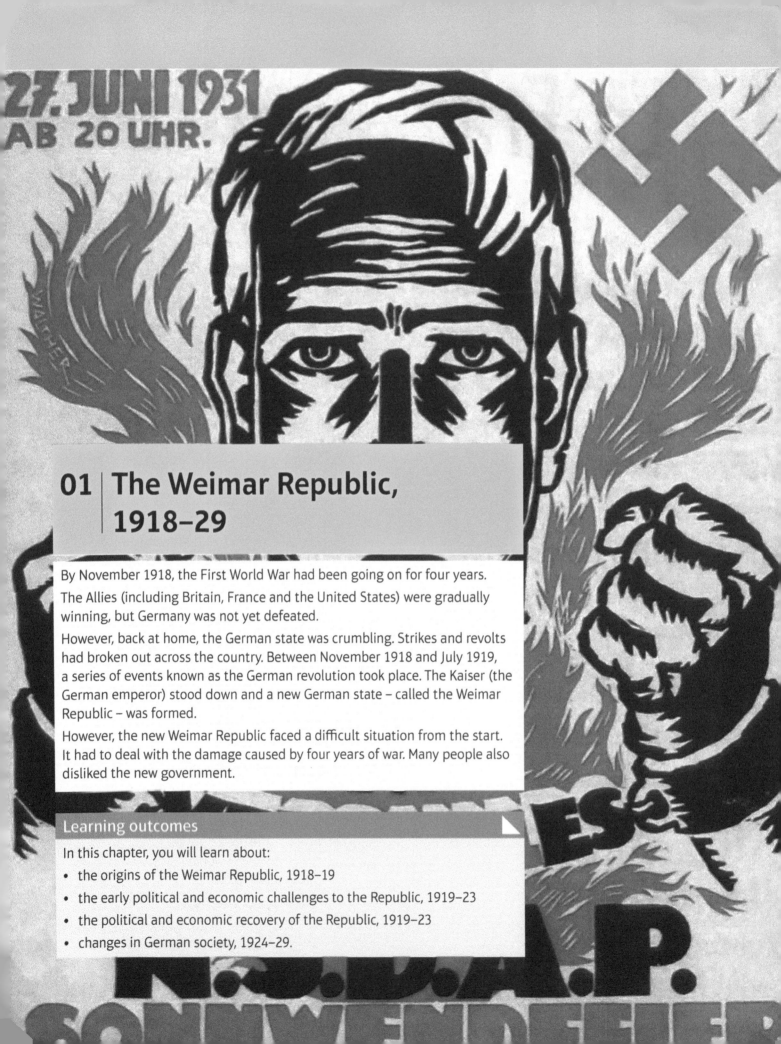

01 | The Weimar Republic, 1918–29

By November 1918, the First World War had been going on for four years.

The Allies (including Britain, France and the United States) were gradually winning, but Germany was not yet defeated.

However, back at home, the German state was crumbling. Strikes and revolts had broken out across the country. Between November 1918 and July 1919, a series of events known as the German revolution took place. The Kaiser (the German emperor) stood down and a new German state – called the Weimar Republic – was formed.

However, the new Weimar Republic faced a difficult situation from the start. It had to deal with the damage caused by four years of war. Many people also disliked the new government.

Learning outcomes

In this chapter, you will learn about:

- the origins of the Weimar Republic, 1918–19
- the early political and economic challenges to the Republic, 1919–23
- the political and economic recovery of the Republic, 1919–23
- changes in German society, 1924–29.

Learning outcomes

- Understand how the end of the First World War affected post-war Germany.
- Examine the beginnings of the Weimar Republic and Weimar Constitution.

The legacy of the First World War

During the First World War, Germany had faced the combined strength of the Allies, which included Britain, France, Russia, Italy and the USA. It had been a long and expensive war.

- Fighting had lasted four years, from 1914 to 1918.
- Eleven million Germans fought in the war. Almost two million German troops died.
- The cost of the war meant that the German government's debts increased from 50 billion marks to 150 billion marks.
- Over 750,000 Germans died because of food shortages.

As a result of this suffering, the German people began to rebel and turn against their government.

Kaiser* Wilhelm (the German emperor) and his government lost control of Germany. It was time for him to go.

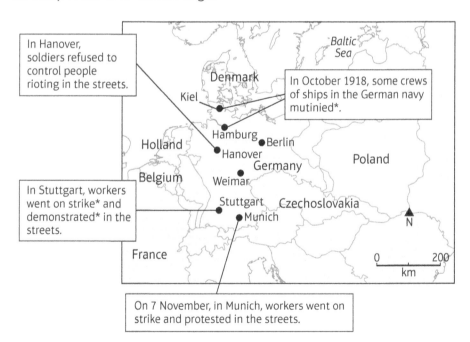

In Hanover, soldiers refused to control people rioting in the streets.

In October 1918, some crews of ships in the German navy mutinied*.

In Stuttgart, workers went on strike* and demonstrated* in the streets.

On 7 November, in Munich, workers went on strike and protested in the streets.

Figure 1.1 A map showing unrest in Germany by November 1918.

Source A

From the papers of Jan Smuts, a South African politician who visited Germany in 1918.

```
... mother-land of our
civilization [Germany] lies
in ruins, exhausted by the
most terrible struggle in
history, with its peoples
broke, starving, despairing,
from sheer nervous
exhaustion, mechanically
struggling forward along the
paths of anarchy [disorder
with no strong authority]
and war.
```

Interpretation 1

From *The Weimar Republic* by John Hiden, published in 1996.

In the face of such pressure, existing order virtually collapsed. The rapid spread throughout Germany of workers' and soldiers' councils confirmed that people were attracted to the prospect of far-reaching political change.

Key terms

Kaiser*

The German emperor.

Strike*

When workers stop work in protest.

Demonstrate*

When people protest against something.

Mutiny*

When people in the military rebel.

The German revolution, 1918–19

By November 1918, the **German revolution** had already begun. Kaiser Wilhelm's government had lost control of the country to strikers and rioters.

The abdication* of the Kaiser

On 9 November 1918, the Kaiser's ministers told him that the only way to restore peace in Germany was for him to give up his position as emperor.

The Kaiser had no choice as he had lost the support of his ministers, the German army, and the German people. On 9 November, he abdicated and, in the early hours of 10 November, he ran away to Holland.

The declaration of a republic

On 9 November, the streets of Berlin were full of people. Some gathered peacefully outside the Reichstag*, while others collected guns and took over parts of the city.

The political party with the most members in the Reichstag was the Social Democratic Party* (SPD). The politicians of the SPD were scared that armed rioters were going to try to take control and set up a communist* government.

Source B

Scheidemann's appeal from the balcony of the Reichstag on 9 November 1918. Scheidemann was a leading SPD politician.

```
The Hohenzollerns [the German royal family]
have abdicated. Take care not to allow
anything to mar this proud day. Long live
the German Republic.
```

Key terms

Abdication*

A leader, like a king, queen or emperor, gives up their position.

Reichstag*

The German parliament.

Social Democratic Party (SPD)*

A moderate party whose politicians were happy that the Kaiser was gone, but did not want the country to fall into chaos, or to communism.

The Council of People's Representatives

Friedrich Ebert, the leader of the SPD, became the first chancellor (like the British prime minister) of the new republic*. He had to work quickly to establish a government.

I will work with the generals of the army to stop the communists from taking power.

I will shut the Reichstag and work with just six politicians – the Council of Representatives – who I completely trust.

We will sign an armistice*, bringing an end to the war.

The Council of Representatives will lead the country until we have written a new constitution*.

Figure: Ebert's immediate aims in 1918.

The armistice

On 11 November, Ebert's representative signed the armistice. This was the formal agreement between Germany and the Allies to end the First World War.

Key terms

Communist*

An extreme form of government, in which representatives of the workers take over ownership of all land, property and resources in a country.

Republic*

A country without a king/queen or emperor/empress.

Armistice*

An agreement made to end a war.

Constitution*

The rules which set out how a country is run.

Setting up the Weimar Republic

The nine months from November 1918 to July 1919 were a tense time for the new republic whilst a new government was put in place. Ebert took several steps to increase people's trust in the new Republic.

Figure: How Ebert won the trust of different groups of people.

Despite Ebert's efforts, some extreme political parties were still unhappy. Demonstrations, and even riots, were common in the major cities.

Still, Ebert had got control, which lasted long enough for a new constitution to be created.

Key terms

Civil servant*

Somebody who works for the government in some way.

Trade unions*

Groups of workers formed to protect the rights and interests of workers in various occupations.

Anarchy*

A country without a government; the word is often used to mean chaotic.

Source C

A German poster from December 1918. The large figure represents the new Republic. The writing says 'Anarchy* Brings Unrest and Hunger'.

Activities

1   List as many points as you can that show that the First World War had weakened the German government (look back at page 9). Here are some clues to help you:

   • In what ways had the war made it harder for the government to rule the country?

   • What was happening in Germany that was difficult for the government to control?

2   The German revolution was a fairly peaceful change of power from the Kaiser to the new republic. Make a list of reasons why the change was fairly peaceful. Consider:

   • why many Germans were glad to see the Kaiser gone

   • why the armistice would have been popular

   • what Ebert did to keep people happy.

The National Assembly

The Council of People's Representatives, which took control of Germany in November 1918, was replaced in January 1919 by the National Assembly. In the elections, moderate parties* gained most of the seats: the SPD won 40%.

The National Assembly met in the town of Weimar as there was too much unrest in Berlin. Its job was to agree a new constitution. The new constitution was agreed on 31 July 1919, and the Weimar Republic was born.

The Weimar Constitution

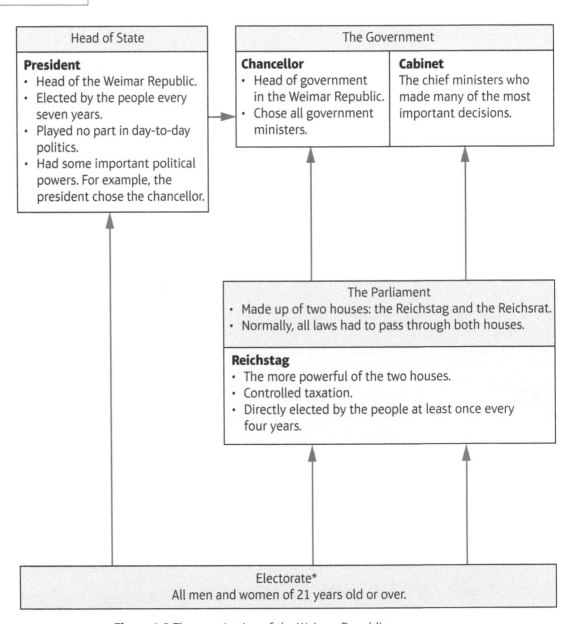

Figure 1.2 The constitution of the Weimar Republic.

The strengths and weaknesses of the Weimar Constitution

The strengths of the constitution

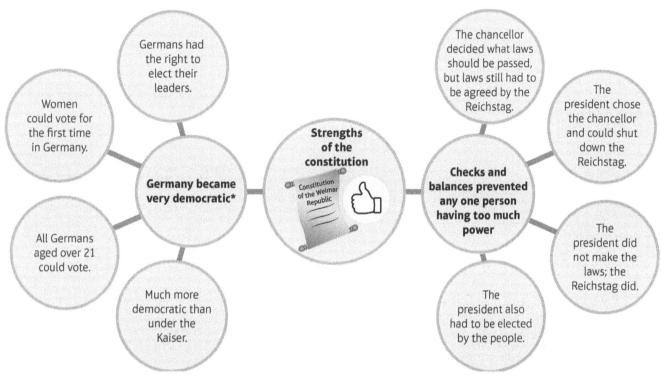

Figure: Strengths of the constitution.

Source D

A photograph, taken on 6 February 1919, showing the official opening of the National Assembly by Friedrich Ebert.

13

The weaknesses of the constitution

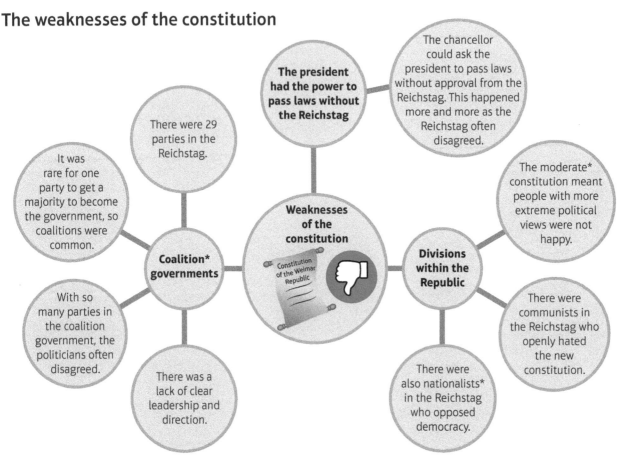

The president had the power to pass laws without the Reichstag

The chancellor could ask the president to pass laws without approval from the Reichstag. This happened more and more as the Reichstag often disagreed.

There were 29 parties in the Reichstag.

It was rare for one party to get a majority to become the government, so coalitions were common.

Weaknesses of the constitution

Constitution of the Weimar Republic

Coalition* governments

With so many parties in the coalition government, the politicians often disagreed.

There was a lack of clear leadership and direction.

Divisions within the Republic

The moderate* constitution meant people with more extreme political views were not happy.

There were communists in the Reichstag who openly hated the new constitution.

There were also nationalists* in the Reichstag who opposed democracy.

Figure: Weaknesses of the constitution.

Activities ?

1 Draw a picture of weighing scales. On one side, write a heading 'Strengths of the Weimar Republic'. On the other side, write a heading 'Weaknesses of the Weimar Republic'. Add what you think are the three most important strengths and three most important weaknesses to the scale. Overall, do you think it was a good constitution?

2 Who do you think was pleased with the new constitution? Who was not?

Key terms

Coalition*

When a government is made up of different political parties.

Moderate*

Not extreme.

Nationalists*

People who strongly love their country.

Source E

A photograph taken at the end of 1918 in Berlin. The building behind the army shows damage caused by rioting.

THINKING HISTORICALLY ▸ Evidence (2b&c)

Different viewpoints

Sometimes people living at the time of great events only know part of what is going on. Their knowledge of events is limited; they see only part of the picture.

This means that what people wrote at the time, and their accounts of the past, sometimes do not give an accurate view about the overall picture of what was happening.

Consider Sources F, G and Interpretation 2. What impression do they give you about how extreme the German revolution was?

Answer the following questions:

1   Sources F and G were produced by people living at the time of the German revolution. What impressions do they give you about how extreme the German revolution was? Do they suggest that there was a big change, or a small one?

2   Interpretation 2 was written by a modern historian. What impressions does it give you about how extreme the German revolution was?

3   Where did the authors of Sources F and G get their information from?

4   Where did the author of Interpretation 2 get their information from?

5   Does Interpretation 2 use information that the people in Sources F and G would not have known?

6   Why do you think that later interpretations sometimes reach different conclusions about events from sources from the time?

Source F

From a description by Rosa Levine-Meyer of events she saw in the streets of Munich in April 1919. Levine-Meyer was a communist leader who set up workers' councils in Munich in 1919 to replace the local government.

The streets were filled with workers, armed and unarmed, who marched by in detachment [groups]... Lorries loaded with armed workers raced through the town, often greeted with jubilant [happy] cheers. The bourgeoisie (the middle classes) had disappeared completely.

Source G

From a description of the German revolution by Anton Pannekoek, a Dutch communist who supported the workers' uprisings in Germany at the end of the First World War, in May 1919.

The result of... the military defeat, was revolution... The masses have destroyed the machinery [old system] that crushed them... they have won political liberty... In Germany the workers have done the same as in Russia – formed Workers' and Soldiers' Councils. These councils... are the new instrument of power for the masses... against the organisation of the middle classes.

Interpretation 2

From *The Coming of the Third Reich* by Richard J. Evans, published in 2004.

Fear and hatred... gun battles, riots and civil unrest... ruled the day in Germany at the end of the First World War. Yet somebody had to take over the reins of power... Radical elements [extreme groups] looked to the workers' and soldiers' councils. [But] instead of revolution, Ebert wanted parliamentary democracy... [rule by an elected parliament – the Reichstag]... Many ordinary electors in Germany saw voting for the three moderate democratic parties as the best way to prevent the creation of a communist revolution. Not surprisingly, therefore, [in January 1919] the Social Democrats, the Democratic Party and the Centre Party gained an overall majority in the elections to the Constituent Assembly. The constitution which it approved in July 1919 was just a modified version of the [old German constitution] established nearly half a century before.

Exam-style question, Section A

Study Source A on page 9.

Give **two** things you can infer from Source A about how well Germany was being governed in November 1918.   **4 marks**

Exam tip

A good answer will select details from the source, for example, 'civilization lies in ruins' or 'its peoples broke, starving, despairing'. It will then explain what these details/quotes from the source suggest about how well Germany was being governed in November 1918. For example, for the quote 'its peoples broke, starving, despairing', you might write that 'This suggests that Germany was being governed badly and that people were suffering due to all the economic problems after the First World War.'

Summary

- With the First World War coming to an end, the Kaiser abdicated on 9 November 1918. The war ended two days later.
- The consequences of the First World War meant that the Social Democratic Party (SPD) had to work quickly to establish control.
- Despite revolts and riots in the streets, Ebert and the SPD established a new government and a National Assembly.
- The National Assembly met in Weimar and created a constitution for the Weimar Republic.
- The constitution had strengths: it was democratic and was meant to stop an individual or party from holding all the power.
- But it also had its weaknesses. Being a coalition, it was weak in a crisis and there were many divisions. This later weakened the Weimar Republic.

Checkpoint

Strengthen

S1 List the ways in which the First World War weakened the German government.

S2 Explain how Ebert kept control of Germany from November 1918 to July 1919.

S3 Describe the key features of the Weimar Constitution.

S4 List the strengths and weaknesses of the Weimar Constitution.

Challenge

C1 How did Germany manage to achieve a fairly peaceful change of power from the Kaiser's leadership to the Weimar Republic?

How confident do you feel about your answers to these questions? If you are unsure, look again at pages 10–11 for C1. If you are still unsure about a question, discuss with others or with your teacher.

Unpopularity of the Republic

The Weimar Republic did not officially start until July 1919, after the armistice and the Treaty of Versailles. However, the leading politicians of the Weimar Republic were the same people who surrendered and signed the unpopular peace treaty, and so they, and the Weimar Republic's government, were blamed for it.

The armistice

On 11 November 1918, just two days after the Kaiser had abdicated, the armistice – an agreement to stop fighting – was signed.

In truth, there was little alternative. By November 1918, Germany was torn apart by unrest and its money and troops were running out (see page 9). But beginning the new republic with a surrender was not a strong start.

The Treaty of Versailles, 1919

Once the **armistice** was signed, the Allied leaders decided the terms of the peace. The peace treaty was eventually signed in a French palace at Versailles, near Paris, on 28 June 1919.

Peace was popular with the German people, as they had suffered during the war. Even so, the terms of the Treaty of Versailles were very unpopular and this also made the Weimar Republic unpopular.

Key term

Allies*

The main Allies were Britain, France and the USA (Russia had pulled out of the war in 1917).

The diktat

Most Germans expected that Germany would be able to negotiate the terms of the peace treaty, but the Allies* refused to allow German representatives to join in the treaty discussions. The treaty was a 'diktat' – meaning the terms were forced upon Germany. The Germans were strongly against the treaty terms.

Source A

A German poster from 1931. It advertises a NSDAP rally and shows a German figure in handcuffs labelled 'Versailles'.

The Treaty of Versailles, 1919

War guilt

Germany was blamed for causing the war. War guilt meant that Germany had to pay reparations* to the countries that won the war. Germany did not agree that it was to blame for causing the war, and Germans hated the war guilt clause*.

Germany lost all its colonies

German colonies* in Africa and Asia were given to the winning nations.

Germany had to pay reparations

The reparations were set at 136,000 million marks (£6.6 billion).

Germany lost land

- Some land in west Germany (including Alsace-Lorraine) was lost and given to France and Belgium.
- Some land in east Germany (including West Prussia) was lost and given to Poland.

- In some areas, people could vote on whether or not they wanted to remain a part of Germany.
- The German port of Danzig was made into an 'international city', not governed by Germany.

These losses meant Germany lost 10% of its population, almost 50% of its iron resources and 15% of its coal.

German military strength was cut

- The German army was limited to 100,000 men.
- Germany was only allowed a small navy.
- No airforce was allowed.
- No German troops were allowed in the Rhineland (an area between France and Germany). It was demilitarised*.

Key terms

Reparations*

When the losing side pays money to cover the cost of war damage.

Clause*

A part of a treaty or agreement.

Colonies*

Land ruled by another country as part of an empire.

Demilitarised zone*

An area where soldiers and weapons are banned.

Economy*

The wealth and resources of a country.

Demilitarised*

An area where troops and military equipment are not allowed.

Figure: Terms of the Treaty of Versailles.

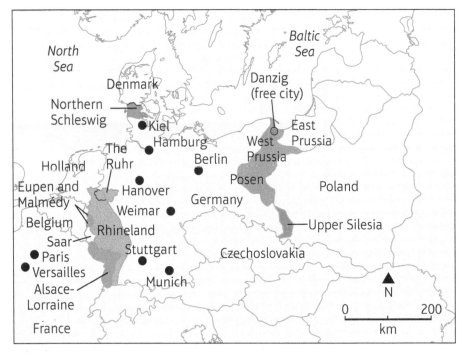

Key

- Areas that Germany had to give to other countries
- Areas that voted to leave Germany
- Demilitarised zone*
- International city

Figure 1.3 Germany and the Treaty of Versailles.

Dolchstoss – the stab in the back

Another reason the Treaty of Versailles was unpopular was because the German people didn't believe their army had been defeated in the war. Although it was in retreat by November 1918, the German army was not defeated. Some people said the army was betrayed by politicians – that they were 'stabbed in the back' (Dolchstoss).

Source B

A poster from 1924 showing a German soldier being 'stabbed in the back'.

Source C

From an article in *Deutsche Zeitung*, a German newspaper, 28 June 1919.

```
Vengeance [revenge], German nation! Today,
in the Hall of Mirrors at Versailles, a
disgraceful treaty is being signed. Never
forget it! On that spot... German honour is
being dragged to its grave. There will be
revenge for the shame of 1919.
```

The impact of the treaty on the Weimar Republic

The Treaty of Versailles aimed to damage Germany's economy*, so that it could not start another world war. This made the Weimar Republic weak from the start.

It also made the Weimar Republic politically weak. The German people were angry with the leaders of the new republic who signed the treaty. They became known as the '**November Criminals**' because they surrendered in November 1918.

Activities ?

1. Play 'Versailles Volleyball'. Divide the class in half and take it in turns to 'lob' a German grievance (complaint) about the Treaty of Versailles 'over the net' to the other team until one side fails to give a different grievance – and loses the game. Jot down each grievance as you play.

2. Consider: the diktat, war guilt, reparations, loss of military strength, lost land, the 'stab in the back'. Which was the biggest grievance? For each grievance, write one or two sentences describing what it was. Then write one or two further sentences explaining why it made people angry.

Interpretation 1 ○

From *The Coming of the Third Reich* by Richard J. Evans, published in 2004.

No one was prepared for the peace terms... All of this was greeted with incredulous horror by the majority of Germans. The sense of outrage and disbelief... was almost universal*. Germany's international strength and prestige had been on an upward course since unification* in 1871... now, suddenly, Germany had been brutally expelled from the ranks of the Great Powers and covered in what they considered to be undeserved shame. Versailles was condemned as a dictated* peace, unilaterally imposed* without the possibility of negotiation.

Key terms

Universal*

Shared or felt by everyone.

Unification*

Before 1871 Germany was a group of separate states. In 1871 these states joined together to form Germany.

Dictated*

To be told what to do.

Unilaterally imposed*

When something is forced on one side by the other side, rather than agreed together.

Challenges to the Weimar Republic from the Left and Right

In the National Assembly (see page 12), which created the constitution for the new republic, most politicians were moderates.

However, there were extreme left-wing and right-wing parties which did not support the Weimar Republic.

Right wing and left wing

Extreme left-wing groups	Moderate parties	Extreme right-wing groups
• Wanted Germany to be controlled by the people. • Wanted to end private ownership of property. • Wanted all business profits to be shared by the workers. • Wanted to co-operate with other countries.	• Supported the Weimar Constitution. • Supported democracy, where people can vote. • Were against extreme changes.	• Wanted Germany to be ruled by a strong leader. • Supported private ownership of property. • Wanted strong law and order. • Wanted Germany to be powerful again.
Example: the German Communist Party.	*Example: the Social Democratic Party.*	*Example: the National Party.*

Figure: What the parties wanted.

The challenge of the Left and Right in the Reichstag

The number of seats* that the moderate parties held in the Reichstag fell greatly between 1919 and 1920. The extremist politicians of the left and the right wings grew in power.

Interpretation 2

From *Nazism and War* by Richard Bessel, published in 2004.

The Social Democratic politicians, into whose lap the German government fell in 1918, didn't have widespread support. Instead, they faced a bitter, suffering population, filled with unrealistic ideas about what peace could bring and divided about… the road ahead.

Activity ?

Study Interpretation 1 and Interpretation 2, which both describe the political situation around 1920. What do they say that is similar, and what information is found in only one of the extracts?

Key term

Seats*

When used to talk about politics, the term 'seats' refers to seats in parliament (the Reichstag in this case). Each politician has one seat.

The main parties of the Weimar Republic

Extremist	Moderate Parties		Extremist	
KPD	SPD	ZP	DNVP	NSDAP
Communist party	**Social Democrats**	**Centre Party**	**National Party**	**Nazi Party**
Extreme left wing	Moderate left wing	Moderate	Right wing	Extreme right wing
Opposed the Weimar Republic	Supported Weimar Republic	Supported Weimar Republic	Unhappily accepted Republic	Opposed Weimar Republic
Supported by workers and some middle classes	Supported by workers and middle classes	Conservatives. Originally the party of the Catholic Church	Landowners, the wealthy and big business	Founded in 1920, eventual main party of Germany in the 1930s

LEFT   RIGHT

Figure 1.4 The main parties of the Weimar Republic.

The challenge of the left and right outside the Reichstag

The Weimar Republic also faced challenges from left and right-wing groups outside of the Reichstag. There were violent uprisings* against the government.

The Spartacist Revolt – a left-wing uprising

- The German Communist Party was set up in December 1918.
- It soon had 33 daily newspapers and 400,000 members.
- The Communists were supported by the Spartacist League.
- The Spartacist League was another extreme left-wing group, based in Berlin.
- It was led by Rosa Luxemburg and Karl Liebknecht.

On 4 January 1919, Ebert sacked the police chief in Berlin. He was popular with the workers. The Spartacists saw this as their chance to attack the government. They called for an uprising and a strike in Berlin. Over 100,000 workers took to the streets. They seized the government's newspaper offices. The Weimar government was losing control of the capital.

The Freikorps

Chancellor Ebert needed to stop the Spartacist rebels. However, the German armed forces were weak after the war, so Ebert had to find soldiers from elsewhere.

Thousands of soldiers released from the army at the end of the First World War had returned to Germany, but had kept their weapons. Many of them hated the communists. Ebert ordered army officers to organise these former soldiers into Freikorps (Free Corps) military units.

The end of the Spartacist Revolt

As the Spartacist Revolt grew, Ebert sent the Freikorps to defeat the rioters. The mainly unarmed workers were no match for the Freikorps soldiers. By 13 January, the rebels had been driven off the streets. Luxemburg and Liebknecht were arrested and killed by Freikorps officers. The left-wing communist rebellion had been defeated.

Source D

A Spartacist poster from the 1920s. The Spartacist champion of the people slays the three-headed monster – the army, big business and landowners – considered by the extreme left wing to be oppressing* the people.

Key terms

Uprising*
An act of resistance or rebellion.

Oppress*
To restrict someone's freedoms or exploit them.

The Kapp Putsch* – a right-wing uprising

The Weimar government had to defend itself against right-wing as well as left-wing unrest. Even the Freikorps turned against the government.

> The Freikorps units were growing very powerful.

↓

> Ebert decided to send home some Freikorps units in order to make the Freikorps less powerful.

↓

> This angered the Freikorps and they turned against the government.

↓

> Five thousand Freikorps rebels took control of Berlin. The Weimar government fled the city.

↓

> The rebels put a right-wing politician called Wolfgang Kapp in control of the city.

↓

> Kapp invited the Kaiser to return to Germany to rule the country.

↓

> The workers of Berlin did not want the Kaiser back so they went on strike. With workers on strike, the city came to a standstill.

↓

> Kapp realised that he could not govern the city and ran away. Because of the actions of the workers, the Kapp Putsch had failed.

Figure: Events of the Kapp Putsch.

The challenge of ongoing political violence 1919–23

Even after the defeat of the Spartacist and Kapp uprisings, political challenges to the Weimar Republic continued from the left and right wings.

There was a series of political assassinations*. For example, **Matthias Erzberger**, the politician who signed the surrender to the Allies in 1918, was killed in August 1921.

Between 1919 and 1922 there were 376 political murders. They were mostly of left-wing or moderate politicians. No right-wing murderer was convicted. Some judges supported the right wing.

Due to all this political violence, most political parties hired armed men to guard their meetings. At first, these private political armies were for protection, but they often caused political meetings and marches to become violent.

The Weimar Republic struggled through the years 1919–22, with threats from left-wing and right-wing extremists. Things would become even worse in 1923.

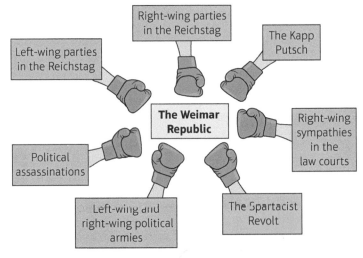

Figure 1.5 The political attacks on the Weimar Republic.

The challenges of 1923

French occupation of the Ruhr

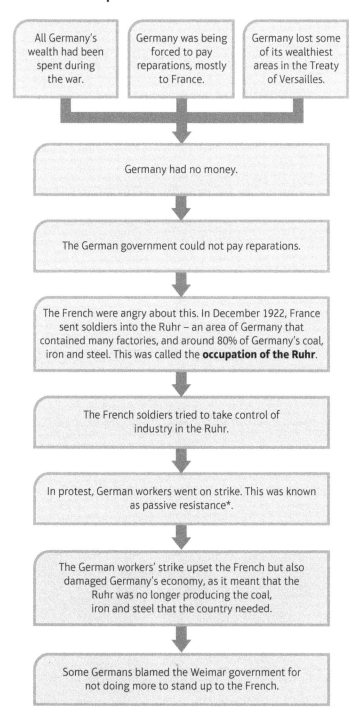

All Germany's wealth had been spent during the war.

Germany was being forced to pay reparations, mostly to France.

Germany lost some of its wealthiest areas in the Treaty of Versailles.

Germany had no money.

The German government could not pay reparations.

The French were angry about this. In December 1922, France sent soldiers into the Ruhr – an area of Germany that contained many factories, and around 80% of Germany's coal, iron and steel. This was called the **occupation of the Ruhr**.

The French soldiers tried to take control of industry in the Ruhr.

In protest, German workers went on strike. This was known as passive resistance*.

The German workers' strike upset the French but also damaged Germany's economy, as it meant that the Ruhr was no longer producing the coal, iron and steel that the country needed.

Some Germans blamed the Weimar government for not doing more to stand up to the French.

Figure: Germany and the occupation of the Ruhr.

Key term

Passive resistance*

To resist something in a non-violent way.

Source E

A poster from Germany in 1923. The figure represents France. The caption reads 'Hands off the Ruhr area!'.

Hände weg vom Ruhrgebiet!

Inflation and hyperinflation

The economic problems in early 1923 meant that the price of things went up – this is called **inflation**. People had to pay more money to get what they needed.

The government needed money to pay its debts. So it printed more money. Printing extra money made it easier for the government to pay reparations, but it also made inflation even worse. The more prices rose, the more money was printed and this made prices rise again. By 1923, prices were incredibly high (see the table below). This extreme inflation is called **hyperinflation**.

Price of a loaf of bread	
1919	1 mark
1922	100 marks
1923	200,000 million marks

The effects of hyperinflation and the damage done

Hyperinflation had many bad effects and some positive effects.

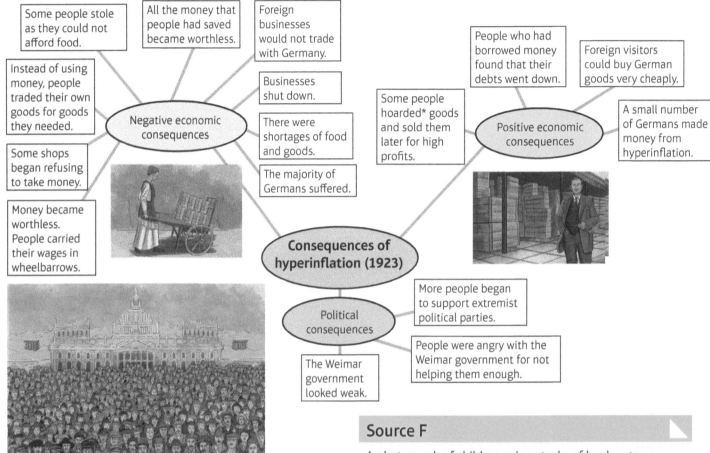

Some people stole as they could not afford food.

All the money that people had saved became worthless.

Foreign businesses would not trade with Germany.

Instead of using money, people traded their own goods for goods they needed.

Businesses shut down.

Negative economic consequences

There were shortages of food and goods.

Some shops began refusing to take money.

The majority of Germans suffered.

Money became worthless. People carried their wages in wheelbarrows.

People who had borrowed money found that their debts went down.

Foreign visitors could buy German goods very cheaply.

Some people hoarded* goods and sold them later for high profits.

Positive economic consequences

A small number of Germans made money from hyperinflation.

Consequences of hyperinflation (1923)

Political consequences

More people began to support extremist political parties.

People were angry with the Weimar government for not helping them enough.

The Weimar government looked weak.

Figure: How hyperinflation affected German people.

Key term

Hoarded*

To stock-up on valuable items to stop other people from getting them.

Source F

A photograph of children using stacks of bank notes as building blocks in Germany in 1923.

Activities ?

1 Working with a partner, create a list of reasons why the German government had run out of money by December 1922. (Hint: think about the consequences of the Treaty of Versailles (see page 18), as well as the figure in Source E on page 23.)

2 Outline the reasons for and effects of the French occupation of the Ruhr.

THINKING HISTORICALLY ▶ Interpretations 2a

The work of the historian

Historians do not aim to tell us about the whole past – they need to choose certain parts of the past to investigate. They do this so that their work is not overloaded with detail. For example, an overview history of the creation of the Weimar Republic might not include witness statements from rioters on the streets, but a work about how the Spartacist Revolt was defeated might contain many such witness statements.

Political unrest in the Weimar Republic 1918–23 – some key information:

55% of German troops in the First World War were killed or wounded.	The price of bread was 200,000 million times higher in 1923 than it was in 1919.	Money put into savings in 1919 was worthless by 1923.
In 1920, Freikorps shot or arrested people who demonstrated in the streets.	Germans believed that their army had been 'stabbed in the back' by the November Criminals.	French occupation of the Ruhr caused many German factories to stop working.
The Allies said that Germany was to blame for the start of the First World War.	In late 1923, if you ordered a coffee for 5,000 marks you could be charged 8,000 by the time you drank it.	Germany was told to pay £6.6 billion in reparations as compensation to the Allies.

Which of the above pieces of information would you use to investigate the following issues? Write out each of the four questions below and then choose two pieces of information from the table for each.

1 How fair were the terms of the Treaty of Versailles?

2 Why was there so much unrest in Germany at the end of 1918?

3 What were the main causes of suffering in Germany 1919–23?

4 What were the effects of hyperinflation in 1923?

With a partner, discuss the following question:

1 Why is it important to carefully choose the information that you put in your historical writing?

Exam-style question, Section A

Explain why there were economic problems in the Weimar Republic from 1919 to 1923.

You may use the following in your answer:

- reparations
- the French occupation of the Ruhr.

You **must** also use information of your own.   **12 marks**

Exam tip

A good answer will:

- include several different things that caused economic problems. Reparations and the occupation of the Ruhr are both mentioned in the question, but you can also include other factors
- contain detailed information about each factor and its economic effects, for example for the occupation of the Ruhr, you might write how it was a very important industrial area for Germany
- explain why each factor caused economic problems. Keep your focus on the question very clear by using words from the question. The phrase, 'This led to economic problems because…' would be one that you could use for each factor.

Summary

- The Treaty of Versailles and the idea that Germans had been 'stabbed in the back' made the Weimar Republic unpopular after 1919.
- From 1919 to 1923, the Weimar Republic was attacked by extreme left-wing and right-wing political groups, inside and outside the Reichstag.
- Examples of these attacks include the Spartacist Revolt and the Kapp Putsch.
- 1923 brought new challenges for the Weimar Republic, such as the French occupation of the Ruhr and hyperinflation.

Checkpoint

Strengthen

S1 List the terms of the Treaty of Versailles which made the Weimar Republic unpopular.

S2 Describe the causes, events and reasons for the failure of the Spartacist Revolt and the Kapp Putsch.

S3 What were the reasons for, and the effects of, the French occupation of the Ruhr?

S4 What were the reasons for, and the effects of, hyperinflation?

Challenge

C1 Explain the reasons for political and economic problems in the Weimar Republic, 1919–23.

How confident do you feel about your answers to these questions? If you are unsure, look again at pages 18–24 for C1. If you are still unsure about a question, join together with others and discuss a joint answer. Your teacher can provide hints.

1.3 The recovery of the Republic, 1924–29

In August 1923, President Ebert appointed Gustav Stresemann as his new chancellor and foreign secretary*. Stresemann resigned the chancellorship in November 1923, but remained as foreign secretary until 1929.

Stresemann's strategy

Stresemann's aims were:

- to make the political situation more stable
- to improve the economy
- to build positive relationships with other countries
- to increase support for moderate political parties
- to reduce support for extreme parties.

Source A

From a speech by Stresemann, describing his support for middle-of-the-road policies in 1924.

I regard it as my duty, as a party man and as a minister, to do all I can to unite the German people for these decisions, and not to force upon them the choice: bourgeois [middle class] or socialist [left wing, e.g. communists].

Reasons for economic recovery

Rentenmark

In November 1923, Stresemann set up a new currency called the **Rentenmark**. The supply of these notes was strictly limited in order to stop inflation*.

Later, in August 1924, a new national bank, called the **Reichsbank**, was given control of this new currency.

The currency was renamed the **Reichsmark**. This solved the problem of inflation, and hyperinflation was at an end.

The Dawes Plan, 1924

In April 1924, an American banker called Charles G. Dawes and Stresemann agreed to a plan to deal with the problem of reparations. It was called the Dawes Plan.

What the Dawes Plan agreed	How the plan helped Germany	Problems caused by the plan
• Reparations were reduced to £50 million per year • US banks would loan huge sums of money to German businesses	✓ Germany could afford reparations ✓ It kept the Allies happy, especially France ✓ It stopped businesses from going bankrupt ✓ Employment and trade increased	✗ Extreme political parties were angry that the Weimar government agreed to pay reparations ✗ Germany was now in huge debt to America ✗ If American banks asked for their money back, Germany would be in trouble

All of this improved the Weimar Republic's economy.

- Industrial output doubled between 1923 and 1928.
- Employment, trade and income from taxation increased.

Key terms

Foreign relations*

The relationships between different countries, such as alliances, treaties and trade deals.

Foreign secretary*

The person within a government who is in charge of foreign relations.

Inflation*

When prices increase.

Activities ?

In pairs, read the following statement by Streseman in 1929: 'The economic position only flourishes [grows] on the surface. Germany dances on a volcano. If loans are called in by the USA, a large section of our economy will collapse.'

What Stresemann meant by this was that the economy of Germany would collapse again if America asked for the money that it had loaned to Germany to be paid back.

1   Using pages 27–28, list four economic changes made from 1923 to 1929.

2   What was the name of the agreement that led to Germany borrowing money from the USA?

3   In what way could Germany borrowing money from the USA be seen to be a bad thing?

Source B

A right-wing cartoon published in 1923. The figure behind the curtain represents the USA. Wall Street was the US financial centre. The caption says 'Here is your enemy'.

The Young Plan, 1929

Five years later, Stresemann agreed to another economic plan: the Young Plan.

What the Young Plan agreed	How the plan helped Germany	Problems caused by the plan
• Total reparations were reduced from £6.6 billion to £2 billion • Germany was given more time to pay (59 years)	✓ Germany now owed less money to the Allies ✓ This meant that the Weimar government could reduce taxes ✓ Lower taxes meant people had more money to buy goods, so industries benefited ✓ Many Germans were happy with the Young Plan and the Weimar government gained popularity	✗ Germany still had to pay £50 million per year ✗ Extreme parties were angry that Germany would be in debt until 1988

Recovery in foreign relations

Stresemann hoped his work in foreign affairs would make the Weimar government more popular in Germany.

The Locarno Pact, 1925

On 1 December 1925, Stresemann signed the Locarno Pact*. This was a treaty between Germany, Britain, France, Italy and Belgium.

Unlike the Versailles Treaty, the Locarno Pact was agreed by Germany, on the same terms with the other main powers.

Figure: Terms of the Locarno Pact.

Stresemann saw this as a major success.

- It made war in Europe less likely.
- Germany was also being treated as an equal.
- The treaty gave Germans more confidence in the Weimar Republic, and increased support for moderate parties.

Source C

A picture from the front of the German magazine *Kladderadatsch* in 1926. The hands represent Germany. The tombstone is labelled Treaty of Versailles. The figures on the top represent Germany's wartime enemies.

The League of Nations

At the end of the First World War, the Allies had set up the League of Nations. This was a new international organisation in which powerful countries discussed ways of solving the world's problems in order to avoid war. At first, Germany was not allowed to join the League. In September 1926, Stresemann got the other countries to accept Germany as a member.

Again, this increased support for the moderate parties which supported Stresemann. However, not all political parties agreed. Some people hated the League and they wanted nothing to do with it. Stresemann disagreed (see Source D).

Source D

An extract from Stresemann's speech on Germany's entry into the League of Nations, 1926.

```
... the League is the product of the treaties
of 1919. Many disputes have arisen between
the League and Germany because of these
treaties. I hope that our co-operation with
the League will make it easier in future to
discuss these questions.
```

Kellogg-Briand Pact

In August 1928, Germany and 61 other countries signed the Kellogg-Briand Pact. This promised that countries would not use war to achieve their aims.

This was another positive step for Germany.

- It showed that Germany was now included amongst the most powerful countries.
- It also showed that the Weimar Republic was now a respected, stable state.
- This increased German people's confidence in the Weimar Republic.

However, not all Germans agreed. The Kellogg-Briand Pact did not remove the hated terms of the Treaty of Versailles, which still limited Germany's power (see Source E).

Source E

A 1929 cartoon, published in Germany, entitled 'Tying Your Friend in Knots'. Briand, the French foreign minister, is on the left, and greets Stresemann as the US president looks on.

The impact on domestic politics

Stresemann had tried to end the hardships of the German people, to cut support for extreme parties and reach agreements with other countries. The impact of his successes is clear. Figure 1.6 shows that support for moderate political parties rose and support for extreme parties fell.

Election results to the Reichstag

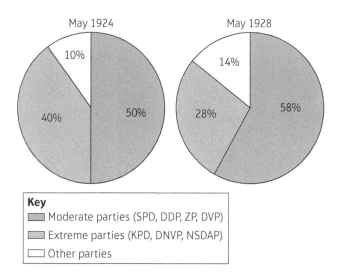

Key
- ▨ Moderate parties (SPD, DDP, ZP, DVP)
- ▥ Extreme parties (KPD, DNVP, NSDAP)
- ☐ Other parties

Figure 1.6 A breakdown of the election results.

The German people's confidence in the Weimar Republic grew in 1925, when President Ebert died. He was replaced by Paul von Hindenburg, a former army general. Hindenburg was very popular and seen as a strong leader.

However, problems were not over for the Weimar Republic. A world economic crisis began in 1929. This led to a new wave of extreme economic and political problems for the Weimar Republic.

Source F

A German journalist, writing in 1929.

In comparison with what we expected after Versailles, Germany has raised herself up. It now shoulders the terrific burden [heavy load] of that peace in a way we should never have thought possible. The bad feeling of Versailles has been conquered [overcome].

Interpretation 1

From a history textbook for schools, published in Britain in 2015.

As the economy improved, so social conditions stabilised and political violence died down. Between 1924 and 1929, no major political figures were assassinated. The Weimar government had been in power for long enough for many people to accept that it was now the political system in Germany – as long as things continued to improve. Support for extremist parties (both left wing and right wing) reduced… Coalition* governments were still the norm, although they changed less often: between 1924 and 1929, there were just six different coalitions. Stresemann's influence was vital to this. However, none of the weaknesses of the constitution had been resolved. And in 1929, Stresemann died.

Activities

1 Create a table, like the one below, to show the ways in which Stresemann's policies between 1923 and 1929 helped Germany to become more stable.

	How the policy helped	Ways in which it didn't
1923 Rentenmark		
Dawes Plan		
Young Plan		
Locarno Pact		
League of Nations		
Kellogg-Briand Pact		

2 Hold a class debate about whether you agree with this statement: 'Between 1923 and 1929, Gustav Stresemann solved the problems of the Weimar Republic'. One half of the class should support the statement and the other half should oppose it.

Key term

Coalition*

A government where different political parties share power.

Exam-style question, Section B

Study Source B (page 28) and Source F (page 31).

How useful are Source B and Source F for an enquiry into the recovery of the Weimar Republic between 1923 and 1929?

Explain your answer, using Source B, Source F and your knowledge of the historical context.   **8 marks**

Exam tip

A good answer will consider:

- how useful the information in each source is for this particular enquiry
- how the provenance (i.e. the type of source, its origin, author or purpose) of each source affects how useful it is
- how knowledge of history at that time affects a judgement of how useful each source is (note that one of the sources was created in 1923, when the situation was very bad, whereas the other was made in 1929, when things had improved slightly).

Summary

- The new currency, introduced in 1923, ended hyperinflation in the Weimar Republic and aided economic recovery in Germany.
- The Dawes Plan and Young Plan reduced the amount of reparations that the Weimar Republic was expected to pay.
- The Locarno Pact, membership of the League of Nations and the Kellogg-Briand Pact marked the return of Germany as a world power. This helped the Weimar Republic to become a respected state.
- However, not all the problems of the Weimar Republic were solved. In 1929, Stresemann died and later that year a new economic crisis began.

Checkpoint

Strengthen

S1 Describe the introduction of the Rentenmark, the Dawes Plan and the Young Plan.

S2 Describe Germany's part in the Locarno Pact, the League of Nations and the Kellogg-Briand Pact.

S3 What economic improvements were there in the Weimar Republic from 1924 to 1929?

Challenge

C1 Explain why the Weimar Republic became more stable from 1924 to 1929.

How confident do you feel about your answers to these questions? If you are unsure, look again at pages 27–29 for S1 and S3, pages 29–30 for S2, and pages 27–31 for C1. If you are still unsure about a question, join together with others and discuss a joint answer. Your teacher can give you hints.

1.4 Changes in society, 1924–29

- Examine the changes in the standard of living for the German people, 1924–29.
- Understand changes for women in the Weimar Republic.
- Understand cultural changes in the Weimar Republic.

Changes in the standard of living

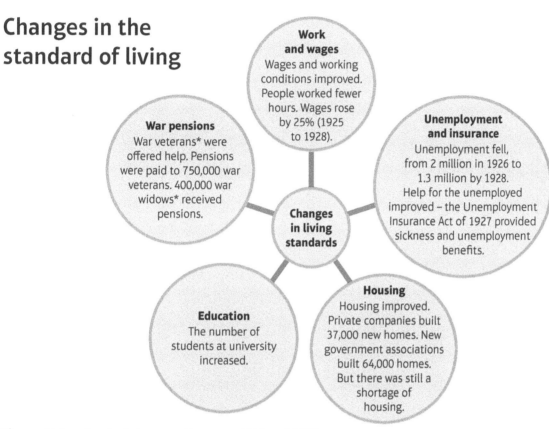

Work and wages
Wages and working conditions improved. People worked fewer hours. Wages rose by 25% (1925 to 1928).

War pensions
War veterans* were offered help. Pensions were paid to 750,000 war veterans. 400,000 war widows* received pensions.

Changes in living standards

Unemployment and insurance
Unemployment fell, from 2 million in 1926 to 1.3 million by 1928. Help for the unemployed improved – the Unemployment Insurance Act of 1927 provided sickness and unemployment benefits.

Education
The number of students at university increased.

Housing
Housing improved. Private companies built 37,000 new homes. New government associations built 64,000 homes. But there was still a shortage of housing.

Figure: Living standards improved between 1918 and 1923.

An improvement in the standard of living?

There were still problems. Jobs were not always permanent. The savings that people had lost during hyperinflation could not be recovered. Not everyone was pleased by the social improvements in 1924–28 (see Interpretation 1).

Interpretation 1

From the History Teachers' Association *Modern History Guide*, published in 2007.

Working people actually improved their situation with better real wages, unemployment insurance and lower working hours. What this did, however, was to alienate* other groups such as big business, who resented their loss of power and profit, and the lower middle class, who saw their own position threatened by a system that seemed to favour the working class.

Key terms

War veteran*
Someone who fought in a war, in this case the First World War.

Widow*
A woman whose husband has died.

Alienate*
To make someone feel left out.

Activities ?

1 'The Weimar Republic brought an improvement in living standards for the German people.' In groups, make a list of evidence to support this statement and a list to oppose it. Draw up a table and write your evidence under these headings: unemployment, wages, housing, education, pensions, the lives of women.

2 Debate this statement in class: 'Weimar Germany brought social change for women.' Note down the key evidence for each side. Write your own view on paper and justify it.

Interpretation 2

From an article on women in Weimar Germany, written by Rudiger Grafin in 2009.

Because of women's improved position in the workforce and their newly acquired rights as citizens... women themselves seemed to have changed... Magazines... presented a new generation of women that differed fundamentally from their mothers.

Changes for women in the Weimar Republic

Women in politics

Women had equal legal rights* to men.

Women were given the right to vote.

Women could become politicians.

90% of women voted in Weimar elections.

By 1932, 10% of the Reichstag were women.

The rights of women

Figure: The rights of women, 1918–32.

Women at work

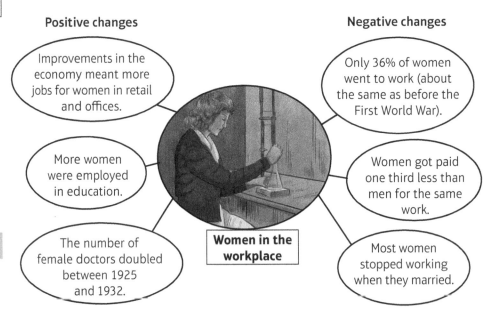

Positive changes

Improvements in the economy meant more jobs for women in retail and offices.

More women were employed in education.

The number of female doctors doubled between 1925 and 1932.

Negative changes

Only 36% of women went to work (about the same as before the First World War).

Women got paid one third less than men for the same work.

Most women stopped working when they married.

Women in the workplace

Figure: There were some improvements for women in the workplace between 1918 and 1932.

Despite improvements, women and men were still not equal in the workplace. Many men opposed women workers and equal pay.

Key term

Legal rights*
Your rights according to the law.

Women at leisure

Figure: 'New women'.

'New women' was the name given to a group of young, wealthier women in the cities, who enjoyed new fashions and opportunities. Images of these 'new women' became common in advertisements and films, but they were not popular with all Germans.

Figure: A conservative/traditionalist*.

Source A

A magazine cover from 1925, comparing a woman from the past (in the foreground) with a 'woman of today' (at the back).

Society divided

People in the Weimar Republic had different feelings about the changes in society:

- some women enjoyed the new opportunities and freedoms; however, other women were scared by the idea that they should change
- some men accepted changing roles for women, others felt that 'new women' threatened their role in society
- some people blamed the economic problems in Germany in the 1920s on women. They said that women were taking the jobs that men needed.

Key term

Conservative/traditionalist*

People who oppose change and want to continue with old traditions.

Cultural changes in the Weimar Republic

A variety of factors led to cultural experimentation* in Weimar Germany.

Interpretation 3

From *Weimar and Nazi Germany*, by Stephen Lee published in 1996.

The 1920s saw a huge cultural revival in Germany. Indeed, these years have been seen as the greatest period of experimentation in the whole of Germany's history. As things settled down politically, writers and artists had more of a chance to try out new ideas. The results were impressive and spread across all areas of the Arts*.

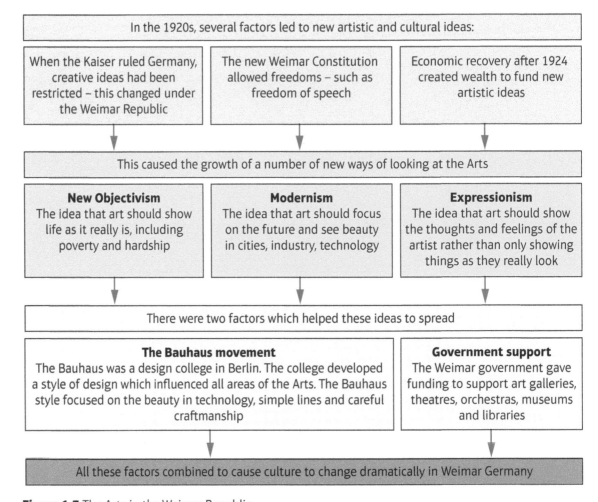

In the 1920s, several factors led to new artistic and cultural ideas:

| When the Kaiser ruled Germany, creative ideas had been restricted – this changed under the Weimar Republic | The new Weimar Constitution allowed freedoms – such as freedom of speech | Economic recovery after 1924 created wealth to fund new artistic ideas |

This caused the growth of a number of new ways of looking at the Arts

New Objectivism
The idea that art should show life as it really is, including poverty and hardship

Modernism
The idea that art should focus on the future and see beauty in cities, industry, technology

Expressionism
The idea that art should show the thoughts and feelings of the artist rather than only showing things as they really look

There were two factors which helped these ideas to spread

The Bauhaus movement
The Bauhaus was a design college in Berlin. The college developed a style of design which influenced all areas of the Arts. The Bauhaus style focused on the beauty in technology, simple lines and careful craftmanship

Government support
The Weimar government gave funding to support art galleries, theatres, orchestras, museums and libraries

All these factors combined to cause culture to change dramatically in Weimar Germany

Figure 1.7 The Arts in the Weimar Republic.

Key terms

Cultural experimentation*

When people come up with new ideas about music, art, film and other creative projects.

The Arts*

A term used to cover many cultural activities, including art, music, theatre and dance.

Art

In art, painters like **Otto Dix** (see Source B) often painted scenes from German life which made German society look very bad.

Source C

A poster for *Metropolis* (1926). It shows an artist's view of the wonders of life in the 20th century.

Source B

A painting by Otto Dix, showing a Berlin street scene, from 1927. It is expressionist in style and shows the harsh life of war veterans and falling standards of behaviour in Germany's night life during the Weimar Republic.

Architecture

Some architects, like **Erich Mendelsohn**, were influenced by the **Bauhaus** school of design. When Mendelsohn was asked to design the **Einstein Tower**, an observatory in Potsdam, he designed a futuristic tower which looks like a rocket. It was unlike anything seen before.

Cinema

Films became popular all over the world in the 1920s. Some German films were very creative and original. *Metropolis*, directed by **Fritz Lang** and released in 1926, was a science fiction film about life and technology in the 20th century. It was partly funded by the government. Germany's first film with sound was made in 1930, and by 1932 there were 3,800 German cinemas showing films with sound.

Opposition

Not everyone agreed with the changes in the Arts. Some people criticised the Weimar Republic.

- Left-wing parties like the KPD said that art funding was a waste, when working people needed basic help.
- Right-wing parties, like the nationalists and the Nazi Party, said the changes went against traditional German culture.

Activities ?

1 Look at Source B on page 37. Write a sentence to explain why this is an example of expressionist art (see page 36 for a definition of expressionism).

2 List reasons why was there was so much cultural change in Weimar Germany in the 1920s (look at Figure 1.7 on page 36).

Exam-style question, Section B

Study Interpretations 2 and 3 on pages 34 and 36. They give different views about the attitudes towards women in Weimar Germany.

What is the main difference between these views?

Explain your answer, using details from both interpretations. **4 marks**

Exam tip

It is not enough just to find differences of detail between the interpretations. The key is:

- to decide how the view in one interpretation is different from the view in the other
- to use details in each interpretation to illustrate how the views differ.

The following sentence starters might be useful:
'Interpretation 2 suggests that women in the Weimar Republic were… This can be seen where it says…'

'However, Interpretation 3 gives a different view. It suggests…'

Summary

- Some improvements in the standard of living took place. However, helping the working classes was not popular with all Germans in the Weimar Republic.
- There were some improvements in the position of women in politics, at work and in leisure. However, the improvements did not go very far and they did not please all Germans.
- Major changes occurred in culture – in art, architecture and the cinema. However, these changes did not please all Germans.

Checkpoint

Strengthen

S1 Give some figures that illustrate changes in unemployment, working hours, wages, housing and the treatment of veterans.

S2 Give examples of how the position of women improved in politics, work and leisure.

S3 Describe the new ideas in the Arts in Weimar Germany and give examples of how these affected art, architecture and cinema.

Challenge

C1 Give your view about whether the standard of living went up for most people in Weimar Germany, using specific details to support your answer.

How confident do you feel about your answers to these questions? If you are unsure, look again at page 33 for S1 and C1, pages 34–35 for S2 and pages 36–38 for S3. If you are still unsure about your answers, join together with others and discuss a joint answer. Your teacher can give you hints.

Recap: The Weimar Republic, 1918–29

Recall quiz

1 Who was the first president of the Weimar Republic?
2 Which political party did he belong to?
3 Who replaced him as president in 1925?
4 Who was the minister responsible for Weimar economic and foreign policy from 1923?
5 In what year did he die?
6 What was the Reichstag?
7 What was the minimum age for voting under the Weimar Constitution?
8 What was the title of the Weimar equivalent of the British prime minister?
9 Under the Weimar Constitution, what power did the president have?
10 What were the initials of the five main political parties in the Weimar Republic?

Activities ?

1 Make a timeline for 1918 and 1919. On the timeline, mark each of the following events. If possible, give the month and year.

  a The abdication of the Kaiser
  b The announcement of the start of the Republic
  c The Council of Representatives take over control of the government
  d The armistice ends the First World War
  e Elections for the National Assembly
  f The National Assembly meets for the first time
  g The Weimar government signs the Treaty of Versailles
  h The new Weimar Constitution is announced

2 Make a list of the reasons why Germans hated the Treaty of Versailles.

3 Divide a sheet of A4 paper into four. Use the four quarters to list key information about each of the following events:

  a the Spartacist Revolt, 1919
  b the Kapp Putsch, 1920
  c the French occupation of the Ruhr, 1923
  d the struggle against inflation, 1923–24.

4 Finish these sentences in as much detail as you can:

  a The Rentenmark was…
  b The Dawes Plan was…
  c The Young Plan was…
  d The Treaty of Locarno was…
  e Joining the League of Nations meant…
  f The Kellogg-Briand Pact was…

5 Give each of the aspects listed below a mark out of 10, to show how much social change it involved. Then write two or three sentences to explain each of your marks.

  a Standards of living
  b The role of women
  c Culture

Writing historically: organising ideas

The most successful historical writing is clearly organised, guiding the reader through the writer's ideas.

Learning outcomes

By the end of this lesson, you will understand how to:

- organise your ideas into paragraphs
- link your paragraphs to guide the reader.

Definition

Paragraph: a unit of text that focuses on a particular point or idea and information related to it.

How can I organise my ideas into paragraphs?

Look at the notes below written in response to this exam-style question:

> Explain why there was opposition in Germany to the Treaty of Versailles (1919). **(12 marks)**

Armistice

Stab in the back – November Criminals

Treaty of Versailles

Diktat

War guilt

Reparations – money had to be paid to allies

Loss military force

Loss total population

Loss of land - colonies

Now look at the full response below.

> There were many reasons why Germans opposed the Treaty of Versailles. Because Germany surrendered, the Treaty of Versailles was a Diktat. This meant that the Germans were given no say in the terms of the treaty, they were not entitled to an opinion. This angered many Germans.
>
> Another reason why Germans opposed the Treaty of Versailles was the 'war guilt' clause. This meant that, since Germany was to blame for the war, it had to pay reparations. Germany had to repay 136,000 million marks to the Allies. It also had to give away land surrounding Germany, such as Alsace and Lorraine as part of the Treaty of Versailles.
>
> A key part of the 'war guilt' clause was reducing the German military. The Allies believed that this would prevent Germany starting another war. The German army was limited to 100,000 men, Germany was the only country made to reduce its military, which the German people opposed.

1. a. What is the key focus of each of these paragraphs (choose from the list on page 40)?

   b. Why do you think this response focused on these key areas?

   c. Why do you think this response put the paragraphs in this order?

   d. Which points in the notes have not been included in the final response (again, look at the list on page 40)? Why do you think the writer decided not to include them?

2. Look closely at the structure of the first paragraph. Which sentences:

   a. show the central topic of the paragraph

   b. show knowledge and understanding of that topic

   c. show that the student is directly answering the question (why there was opposition to the Treaty of Versailles)?

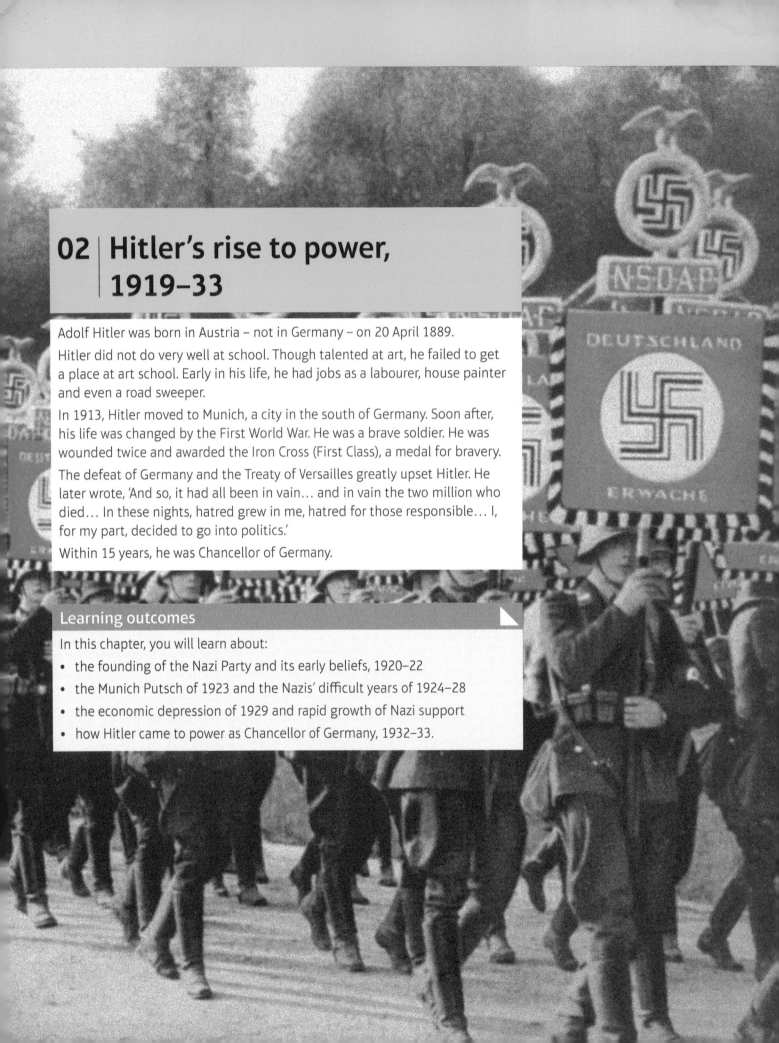

02 | Hitler's rise to power, 1919–33

Adolf Hitler was born in Austria – not in Germany – on 20 April 1889.

Hitler did not do very well at school. Though talented at art, he failed to get a place at art school. Early in his life, he had jobs as a labourer, house painter and even a road sweeper.

In 1913, Hitler moved to Munich, a city in the south of Germany. Soon after, his life was changed by the First World War. He was a brave soldier. He was wounded twice and awarded the Iron Cross (First Class), a medal for bravery.

The defeat of Germany and the Treaty of Versailles greatly upset Hitler. He later wrote, 'And so, it had all been in vain… and in vain the two million who died… In these nights, hatred grew in me, hatred for those responsible… I, for my part, decided to go into politics.'

Within 15 years, he was Chancellor of Germany.

Learning outcomes

In this chapter, you will learn about:

- the founding of the Nazi Party and its early beliefs, 1920–22
- the Munich Putsch of 1923 and the Nazis' difficult years of 1924–28
- the economic depression of 1929 and rapid growth of Nazi support
- how Hitler came to power as Chancellor of Germany, 1932–33.

Hitler's early career in politics

After the First World War, Adolf Hitler was employed by the army to watch what the local political activists* were doing in Munich. As part of this work, Hitler began to attend the meetings of the German Workers' Party (DAP).

Hitler joins the German Worker's Party (DAP)

The DAP had been founded in Munich in February 1919. It was tiny – at the first meeting attended by Hitler, on 12 September 1919, there were only 23 people. Even so, Hitler liked the party's ideas and he joined the DAP.

Setting up the Nazi Party (NSDAP)

Within two years, Hitler had taken control of the DAP and reshaped it into the Nazi Party. There were five parts to this takeover:

- party policy
- Hitler's personal appeal
- party organisation
- party leadership
- the *Sturmabteilung* (SA) or 'Brownshirts'.

Party policy – the Twenty-Five Point Programme

Hitler began to take control of the policies of the DAP. It was strongly against:

- the **Weimar politicians** who overthrew the Kaiser, made peace and accepted the Versailles Treaty
- democracy*, which they believed to be weak, and the Weimar Constitution
- the **Jews**, whom they blamed for weakening the German economy.

In January 1920, Hitler became head of party propaganda*. In February, Hitler wrote the party's Twenty-Five Point Programme, a document explaining the policies of the DAP (see Source A).

Key terms

Activist*

Someone who campaigns for change.

Democracy*

Where people have the right to elect their leaders.

Propaganda*

A way of controlling public attitudes. Propaganda uses things like newspapers, posters, radio and film, to put ideas into people's minds and therefore shape attitudes.

Reich*

The German word for 'empire'.

Source A

Extracts from the Twenty-Five Point Programme, originally produced by the DAP in February 1920.

1 We demand the union of all Germans in a Greater Germany.

2 We demand equality of rights for the German people in its dealings with other nations.

3 We demand land and colonies to feed our people and settle our surplus population [extra people].

4 Only those of German blood... are members of the nation. No Jew may be a member of the nation.

7 We demand that the State's primary duty must be to promote work and the livelihood of its citizens.

9 All citizens shall have equal rights and equal duties.

17 We demand... a law to take from the owners any land needed for the common good of the people.

22 We demand... the creation of a people's army.

25 We demand the creation of a strong central state power for the Reich*.

Interpretation 1

From *Weimar and Nazi Germany*, by Stephen Lee, in 1996.

The [Twenty-Five Point] programme contained policies which may be described as either nationalist* or socialist*, or both. The nationalist policies emphasised race, expansion, the army, power and relations with other countries. The socialist policies were to do with state controls over the living conditions of the people and the economy.

Hitler's personal appeal

Hitler's personal appeal* as an orator (public speaker) attracted a lot of support.

- His speeches were carefully practised.
- He used strong body language, such as waving his arms about, to make a point.
- He was very persuasive.
- His speeches started quietly before building to a loud finish.
- He spoke with passion about the things that were important to him.

Figure: Hitler's skills as an orator.

Key terms

Nationalist*

A political outlook which aims to make the nation stronger and more independent.

Socialist*

A political outlook which stresses that a country's land, industries and wealth should all belong to the workers of that country.

Appeal*

Attractive qualities that make someone likeable.

Auditorium*

A large hall with seating for an audience.

As Hitler's appeal became known, membership of the DAP grew to 3,000 by the end of 1920. Most of the new members were Hitler's followers.

Source B

A quotation from a supporter at a Nazi Party meeting in 1926.

A wave of jubilation [joy], rising from afar, moving into the lobby announced the arrival of the Führer [leader]. And then the auditorium* went wild. When the speech came to an end... there were tears in my eyes... others, men, women and youngsters were as deeply affected as I.

Activities ?

Consider Source B.

1 What does this quotation tell you about Hitler's popularity within the DAP?

2 Do you think all Germans would have shared this view of Hitler? Explain your answer.

Source C

A painting by Hermann Hoyer. It was exhibited by Adolf Hitler at the Great German Art Exhibition in 1937. It is entitled 'In the beginning there was the word' and shows Hitler addressing a party meeting in 1921.

Party organisation

As the DAP party's leader of propaganda, Hitler introduced a number of changes.

The DAP set up an office in Munich. The party's meetings were now better organised and well advertised. Party membership and funds began to increase.

'Nationalsozialistische'

National Socialist

Hitler suggested renaming the party to the National Socialist German Workers' Party (NSDAP – or 'Nazi' Party for short).

The three parts of the name – national, socialist and workers – appealed to many different people. The party became more popular.

The NSDAP was easily recognisable from its logo, the swastika, and its straight-armed party salute.

The NSDAP bought a newspaper – the Völkischer Beobachter (the 'People's Observer'). This meant the views of the NSDAP could now spread to far more people.

Figure: Changes in the organisation of the party.

Interpretation 2

An extract from *The Weimar Republic*, by John Hiden, published in 1996.

The NSDAP was built up not only on protest but on resentment [anger]. This is evident from its programme as well as… the party's chief followers and leading officials. Hitler incorporated in his own person many of the major features on which his movement [the NSDAP] thrived: the deep sense of frustration, hate against Jews and Marxists (communists)… dislike of parliamentary democracy. To build up a mass movement from such beginnings and keep it together required unique personal qualities. It was clear, for example, from the very beginning that the NSDAP depended heavily on Hitler's spectacular speaking skills.

Party leadership

In July 1921, Hitler became leader of the NSDAP. He surrounded himself with supporters to help him lead the party. They included:

- **Rudolf Hess**, a wealthy academic, who became Hitler's deputy
- **Hermann Goering**, a young, and wealthy First World War fighter pilot
- **Julius Streicher**, a publisher who started another Nazi newspaper, *Der Stürmer* ('The Stormer')
- **Ernst Röhm**, a ex-army officer who was popular amongst ex-soldiers.

Hitler also made powerful friends such as General Ludendorff, leader of the German Army during the First World War.

The role of the SA (Sturmabteilung)

Sturmabteilung, or stormtroopers, were another way that Hitler kept control of the party.

Figure: Hitler's stormtroopers.

The SA showed their power and importance by marching around the streets. By August 1922, they numbered about 800. At NSDAP meetings, the SA was used to control the crowds, stopping any opposition to Hitler, often with violence. They were also sent to stop the meetings of other political groups.

Source D

A photograph of the SA on parade, displaying their brown uniforms and the swastika. The flags say, 'Germany awake'.

The SA strengthened Hitler's position. Although Ernst Röhm was put in charge of the SA, Hitler expected them to obey him. Many of the SA were violent and hard to control so Hitler chose the more trusted ones as his own bodyguards and they were known as the Stosstrupp, or Shock Troop.

Hitler gains complete control of the NSDAP

By the party conference of January 1922, Hitler's control of the NSDAP was complete. He persuaded the members to give up their right to elect their leader. The NSDAP was his party.

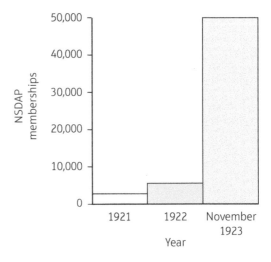

Figure 2.1 Membership figures of the NSDAP.

Interpretation 3

From an article by Gerhard Rempel on Hitler's style of leadership.

The congress [party conference] was a mile-stone in the organisational history of the NSDAP because it marked the beginning of Hitler's complete, personalised control of the party's... organisational structure... Hitler persuaded the membership to give up voluntarily the rights it had enjoyed under the democratic rules of the NSDAP and to accept instead a framework of discipline and obedience to himself. In turn he promised that his personalised control of the NSDAP would enable the party to play a more effective part in felling [bringing down] the Weimar Republic.

THINKING HISTORICALLY Interpretations (2b)

The importance of perspective

What historians 'see' is shaped by what they are interested in and what they see as important. Historians also sometimes use different methods of investigating and will consider sources in different ways.

Consider the following question, for example:

How far was the growth of the NSDAP caused by popular support for its policies and how far was it caused by popular support for Hitler, its leader?

	Conceptual* approach	Methodology*
Historian A	Historian A believes ideas shape history. He believes that powerful feelings, like anger against something, can shape what people want and powerful ideas like nationalism and communism can shape what they do.	Historian A looks at the bigger picture. For Weimar Germany, he studies the Versailles peace treaty, economic problems in Germany, examples of political unrest across the country. He sees these things as influencing events.
Historian B	Historian B thinks people control events. She believes that events are shaped by the choices a nation's people make and by the actions and personality of key individuals, like Hitler.	Historian B uses local sources. She studies what happened to the NSDAP in Munich, the minutes of its meetings, the articles in its newspapers. She reads about Hitler and the opinions of the people who saw Hitler speak.

Answer the following:

a What answer do you think Historian A would give to the question?

b What answer would Historian B give?

c What facts would Historian A use to back up his argument?

d How would the facts used by Historian B differ from this?

e Do these approaches mean that one historian is wrong and the other right? Explain your answer.

f What does this activity tell you about why interpretations in history differ?

Activities ?

1 Look at pages 43–44. Interpretation 1 says that the key policies of the DAP were nationalism and socialism. Pick out statements from the DAP's Twenty-Five Point Programme in Source A which show i) nationalism and ii) socialism (see definitions on page 44).

2 Use pages 43–46 to make a list of Hitler's personal qualities. Next to each, write a sentence or two to explain how this quality helped him to take control of the NSDAP.

3 Hitler used five strategies to take control of the NSDAP: controlling party policy, personal appeal, controlling party organisation, his leadership takeover and control of the SA.

    a Write a short paragraph to summarise each of the five strategies.

    b Write one paragraph to explain which was the most important.

Key terms

Conceptual*

The way someone thinks.

Methodology*

The way someone works.

Exam-style question, Section A

Give **two** things you can infer from Source A (page 43) about the NSDAP in the 1920s.   **4 marks**

Exam tip

This question tests source analysis, specifically the skill of making inferences.

A good answer will suggest something that can be inferred from the source and then back this up with details or quotes from the source.

For example, you might write, 'Source A suggests the NSDAP were… because the source says…'

This would need to be repeated.

Summary

- Hitler joined the DAP in September 1919.
- Between 1919 and 1923, Hitler took control of the DAP.
- Hitler took over by controlling party policy, using his personal appeal, controlling party organisation, winning the leadership and using the SA.
- Hitler changed the DAP into the NSDAP with easily recognisable features, such as the swastika, the straight-armed salute and the SA.

Checkpoint

Strengthen

S1 Describe Hitler's first experiences of the DAP.

S2 Describe the policies that Hitler set out for the DAP in the Twenty-Five Point Programme.

S3 Explain Hitler's personal appeal to new party members.

S4 Describe the changes Hitler made to the DAP as he created the NSDAP.

S5 Describe how Hitler created the SA to strengthen himself and the NSDAP.

S6 Describe the growth in membership of the NSDAP, 1920–23.

Challenge

C1 Explain how far the growth of the NSDAP was due to its policies and how far it was due to Hitler.

How confident do you feel about your answers to these questions? If you are unsure, look again at pages 43–46 for S1–S6; for C1 you could discuss the answer with other people. Your teacher can provide hints.

The Munich Putsch, 1923

In November 1923, Hitler launched the Munich Putsch*, sometimes called the Beer Hall Putsch. It was an armed revolt intended to overthrow the Weimar Republic.

Reasons for the Munich Putsch

A mix of long-, medium- and short-term causes brought about the Munich Putsch.

Key terms

Putsch*
A violent uprising intended to overthrow existing leaders.

Fascist*
A political ideology that considers the nation more important than the individual.

Patriotic*
Being very loyal to, or proud of your country.

Fever pitch*
Extreme excitement.

Long-term causes

Some Germans were angry with the leaders of the Weimar Republic. They hated the Treaty of Versailles. This led to support for nationalist parties like the NSDAP. From 1919 to 1923, the NSDAP grew in popularity, especially in Munich and Bavaria, in southern Germany. By 1923, they had 50,000 members.

Medium-term causes

From 1921, Hitler and the NSDAP were inspired by a right-wing party in Italy, called the Fascists. In 1922, that party's leader Mussolini led his supporters in a 'march on Rome', where he made the government of Italy accept him as their new leader.

Interpretation 1

From *The Coming of the Third Reich*, by Richard J. Evans, published in 2004.

The 'march on Rome' galvanised [motivated] the fascist* movements of Europe… As the situation in Germany began to deteriorate… Hitler began to think that he could do the same in Germany as Mussolini had done in Italy.

Short-term causes

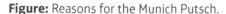

During 1923, hyperinflation reached its peak (see page 23). Buying everyday goods became almost impossible. French troops entered the German industrial area of the Ruhr. The German people were very angry about these events. Hitler felt that it was the right time to take advantage of the anger of the people and so, in November 1923, he made an attempt to take power.

Source A

From a report in September 1923 by the Bavarian police.

As a result of rising prices and unemployment, the workers are bitter. The patriotic* are at fever pitch* because of the failure of the resistance in the Ruhr.

Figure: Reasons for the Munich Putsch.

The events of the Munich Putsch

On the evening of 8 November 1923, Bavarian government officials were meeting in a beer hall, in Munich.

Gustav von Kahr, the leader of the state government of Bavaria, was the main speaker.

---

8 November, 1923, evening

Hitler and 600 SA soldiers burst into the beer hall. Hitler was supported by General Ludendorff, the famous First World War general.

Hitler said that he was taking control of Bavaria and would then march to Berlin to overthrow the Weimar Republic.

At gunpoint, Hitler forced Kahr and the other government ministers to agree to support him.

↓

8 November, night

While Hitler was organising his supporters, Ludendorff let Kahr leave the beer hall. Kahr withdrew his support for Hitler and began organising opposition to the Putch.

↓

9 November

Hitler decided to take his revolt to the streets of Munich, where 1,000 SA soldiers were joined by another 2,000 volunteers. They began marching through the city.

Hitler hoped that he would be supported by the local people. Most, however, did not want to join his Putsch.

The Nazi supporters were met by the local police and army forces, who were better armed than the SA.

Violence broke out. Fourteen Nazi supporters and four policemen were killed. The rebels fled.

Ludendorff was arrested. Hitler fled and went into hiding in a house.

↓

11 November

Hitler was found and arrested.

The Munich Putsch had failed.

Figure: The Munich Putsch – a timeline.

Source B

An announcement made on 9 November 1923 by Gustav von Kahr, leader of the state government of Bavaria.

The deception and treachery* of ambitious rebels have changed a peaceful meeting, held to encourage people to work together, into a scene of disgusting violence. The declarations of support, forced from myself, General von Lossow and Colonel Seisser at the point of the gun, are null and void*. The National Socialist German Workers' Party (NSDAP), and the troops who have gathered to support them, are banned.

Source C

A photograph of Hitler's Shock Troop in Munich on the morning of the Putsch, 8 November 1923.

Key terms

Treachery*

Betraying a person or your country.

Null and void*

Does not count for anything.

Source D

A painting from 1940 by H. Schmitt, one of Hitler's followers, who took part in the Munich Putsch. Hitler stands at the front of the rebels with his arm raised, with Ludendorff on his right.

Interpretation 2

From *Adolf Hitler* by John Tolund, published in 1996.

The state police rounded up hundreds [of rebels], disarming them on the street. The rebels left behind at the beer hall to hold the command post were so unstrung [unsettled] by the catastrophe that they surrendered without resistance to police. They stacked up their arms and went home to brood. The Putsch was over. But victorious state police marching away from the beer hall were abused by indignant* citizens, with cries of "Betrayers of the Fatherland! Jew defenders! Bloodhounds! Heil* Hitler – Down with Kahr!"

Activity ?

What does Interpretation 2 tell you about:

a the armed rebels who supported Hitler

b support for the revolt in the general population of Munich?

Key terms

Indignant*

Feeling angry when you think you have been treated unfairly.

Heil*

A German greeting of respect.

Activities

1   Make a list of the causes of the Munich Putsch, then hold a class debate about what you believe to have been the main cause.

2   Draw a timeline covering 8 to 11 November 1923. Mark on it the key events of the Munich Putsch.

3   Look at Source D on page 51.

    a   What impression does it give you about Hitler's part in the Munich Putsch?

    b   Why do you think it shows Hitler like this? (Hint: consider who created the image.)

4   Look at Source E.

    a   What is Hitler doing in the image?

    b   Does this artist think that Kahr supported Hitler, or opposed him?

Key term

Arsonist*

Someone who intentionally sets fire to things illegally.

Exam-style question, Section A

Explain why the Munich Putsch (1923) failed.

You may use the following in your answer:

• the German army

• Bavarian leaders.

You **must** also use information of your own.   **12 marks**

Source E

A 1924 cartoon from the political magazine *Simplicissimus*. Hitler is shown setting fire to the town. He is being carried by von Lossow, the head of the German Army in Bavaria, and von Kahr, the leader of the state government of Bavaria. Meanwhile, Kahr shouts out: 'Officer, arrest that arsonist* up there.'

Exam tip

A good answer will:

• include several factors that were reasons for failure. Two factors have been given for you: the German army and the Bavarian leaders. Try to think of a third factor.

• contain detailed information about each factor and how it weakened the revolt. For the Bavarian leaders, you might include their names and details of what they did.

Ensure that you directly answer the question. You could use the phrase, 'This led to the failure of the Munich Putsch because…'

THINKING HISTORICALLY Interpretations (4a)

The weight of evidence

Historians' interpretations are not simply their opinions. Interpretations are theories (sets of ideas). In order for theories to be strong, they need to be backed up with solid evidence.

When you write your own interpretations of historical events, you too should be using evidence to make your conclusions as strong as possible.

Below, there are three 'Conclusions' that students have written about Hitler's reasons for the Munich Putsch. They are based on Source F.

Work in pairs. Read Source F and the three conclusions below, then answer the questions.

Conclusion 1

Hitler planned the Munich Putsch because he wanted power for himself. This is clear because he says, 'the national government will be taken over by me'.

Conclusion 2

Hitler planned the Munich Putsch because he wanted a stronger Germany. We know this because he said he would replace the 'wretched Germany of today' with a Germany of 'greatness, freedom and splendour'. Further evidence is that Hitler's first appointments are the leaders of the armed forces, the army, the police; this shows he wanted a strong Germany. Finally, Hitler saying that the Bavarian prime minister would have dictatorial powers shows that he wanted a strong Germany.

Conclusion 3

Hitler planned the Munich Putsch because he wanted right-wing government in Germany. He proposed a Regent, or temporary monarch, in Bavaria. He also proposed a Bavarian prime minister with dictatorial powers.

1 Write out each conclusion and then use highlighter pens to colour code them. Use one colour for 'evidence', another colour for 'conclusions' and a third for language that shows 'reasoning' (e.g. "therefore", "so").

2 How are the conclusions different in the way they use evidence?

3 Put the conclusions in order from the best to the worst.

4 What do you know about the Munich Putsch? Is there any more evidence that could be used to back up each conclusion? Add it to the conclusions.

5 Write your own conclusion using evidence from the source and your own knowledge.

Source F

An extract from a speech made by Adolf Hitler at the Bergerbrau Keller on the evening of 8 November 1923.

The Bavarian government is removed. I propose that a new Bavarian government shall be formed consisting of a Regent [a temporary monarch] and a Prime Minister who will have dictatorial* powers. I propose Herr von Kahr as Regent and Herr Pohner as Prime Minister.

The national government of the November Criminals* and the Reich President in Berlin are declared to be removed. I propose that, until we can bring the November criminals to account, the national government will be taken over by me. Ludendorff will take over the leadership of the German National Army, Lossow will be German Minister for the Armed Forces, Seisser will be the German Police Minister.

I want now to fulfil the vow which I made to myself five years ago when I was a blind cripple in the military hospital: to know neither rest nor peace until the November criminals had been overthrown, until on the ruins of the wretched* Germany of today there should have arisen once more a Germany of power and greatness, freedom and splendour.

Key terms

Dictatorial*
Where someone tells someone what to do, without discussion or democracy.

Wretched*
Poor and hopeless. In bad condition.

November Criminals*
The insulting nickname given to the German politicians (some of whom later became politicians in the Weimar Republic) who signed Germany's surrender at the end of the First World War.

Interpretation 3

From *The Coming of the Third Reich*, by Richard J. Evans, published in 2004.

It seems likely that they (the Bavarian authorities) offered Hitler leniency [mercy] in return for his agreement to carry the can [take responsibility]. As judge, they picked… a well-known nationalist… Hitler was allowed to wear his Iron Cross and address the court for hours on end… The court grounded its leniency in the fact that the participants *'were led in their action by pure patriotic spirit and noble will'*. **The judgement was scandalous [shocking] even by the standards of the Weimar judiciary*.**

Source G

From a letter, written by Hitler in 1924, while in prison after the Munich Putsch.

When I resume active work, it will be necessary to pursue a new policy. Instead of working to achieve power by an armed coup*, we will have to hold our noses and enter the Reichstag. If outvoting them takes longer than outshooting them, at least the result will be guaranteed by their own constitution. Sooner or later we shall have a majority, and after that – Germany!

Key terms

Judiciary*
The courts system.

Coup*
An attempt to overthrow a government.

Treason*
To betray your country.

Consequences of the Munich Putsch

Hitler and several other leaders of the Putsch were put on trial.

- Ludendorff was found not guilty – more because of the support of the judge rather than the evidence.
- Hitler and three others were found guilty of treason* and sentenced to five years in Landsberg Prison.
- The NSDAP was banned.

In the short term, the Munich Putsch was a defeat for Hitler, although he was released after only nine months. However, in the longer term, the results were not all bad for him.

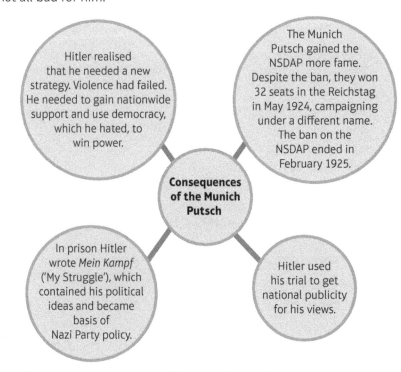

Figure 2.2 Consequences of the Munich Putsch.

Activity

Consider the results of the Munich Putsch.

a Draw a table with two columns, as below, and complete it using your knowledge of the Munich Putsch.

Ways the Munich Putsch was a failure for the Nazis	Ways the Munich Putsch was a success for the Nazis

b Make a judgement: overall, was the Munich Putsch a failure or a success? Write two or three sentences to justify your judgement.

The lean years of the Nazi Party, 1924–28

Mein Kampf

Hitler used his time in prison to read and write. He wrote down his ideas in his book *Mein Kampf* (My Struggle).

Mein Kampf is a key source of information about the political beliefs of Hitler's Nazi Party after 1924. For example, *Mein Kampf* makes Hitler's extreme racist views very clear.

Ideas about race
- The German race (which Hitler called the Aryan race) should rule the world.
- Jews were trying to stop Aryan rule.
- Jews were taking over Aryan businesses and the moderate political parties.

Traditional values
- A woman's role should be as a wife and mother. A man's role should be as a worker and soldier.
- Support Christian values.
- No modern music or art, only traditional German music and art.

Nationalism
- Make Germany powerful again.
- Reverse the Treaty of Versailles.
- Gain more living space for Aryan people by invading other countries.

Key ideas in *Mein Kampf*

Totalitarianism
- Get rid of democracy.
- Replace democracy with a dictatorship*.

Socialism
- Use the wealth of businesses to help ordinary German people.
- Stop rich landowners and business owners from keeping their wealth to themselves.

Figure: Hitler's ideas from *Mein Kampf*.

Source H

A NSDAP campaign poster from 1924. It emphasises Nazi principles of family, work and nationalism.

Party reorganisation, 1924–28

- Hitler was released from prison on 20 December 1924, after just nine months of his five-year sentence.
- The ban on the NSDAP was lifted on 16 February 1925.
- Hitler was able to relaunch the NSDAP at a meeting in Munich on 27 February that year.
- The treatment of Hitler and the Nazi Party was typical of the way the law courts dealt with violent right-wing attacks on the Weimar Republic.

However, the failure of the Munich Putsch had persuaded Hitler that he could not rely on violence to take control of Germany. He had to be elected to power. He therefore made the Nazis a much better-organised political party.

Key term

Dictatorship*

Government by a single ruler who has complete power.

Nazi Party headquarters

The central base of the Nazi Party was at its party headquarters in Munich.

- The party was organised like a mini state, with Hitler as the leader and departments for all aspects of government, such as finance, foreign affairs, industry, agriculture and education.
- The party had a women's section called The German Women's Order. There was also a National Socialist German Students' League for 14 to 18 year-olds, known as the Hitler Youth.

The creation of a national Nazi Party

The rest of Germany was divided into 35 regions or *Gaue*. Each *Gau* had a leader, or *Gauleiter*, the local leader of the Nazi Party. **Joseph Goebbels**, who would later become one of the most important Nazis, was a Gauleiter for the Rhineland region.

To pay for all this, Hitler changed the party finances. He raised money from wealthy industrialists* who shared some of Hitler's views.

The Schutzstaffel or SS

By 1930, the SA had 400,000 members. But Hitler did not trust them. The SA were difficult to control, and they were loyal to their commander, Ernst Röhm.

In 1925, Hitler began to tighten his control of the SA.

- He replaced Röhm as leader of the SA.
- He set up the *Schutzstaffel* (protection squad) – the SS. It was a smaller group with hand-picked members, whom Hitler trusted to protect him. Hitler placed the SS under the control of Heinrich Himmler, a senior member of the Nazi Party.

Key term

Industrialist*
Someone who owns or runs industry.

Source I

A photograph of a parade of SS members in Nuremberg in 1933.

The Bamberg Conference of 1926

By early 1926, it was clear that the local power of *Gauleiters* was creating a split in the Nazi Party.

- Some party members, such as Goebbels, emphasised the **socialist** part of National Socialism. They wanted benefits for workers and attacks on businessmen and landowners.
- But other party leaders, such as Hitler himself, emphasised the **nationalist** part of National Socialism. They wanted a strong German state and action against the Jews.

To sort out the split, Hitler set up a Nazi Party conference. They met in Bamberg, in Bavaria.

What happened at the Bamberg Conference	Results of the conference
• Hitler spoke for 5 hours. He made his views clear. He tried to show that the 'socialist' part of the party were similar to communists – the enemies of the Nazis. • Hitler tried to win over Goebbels to his side.	• Hitler had clear control of the Nazi Party. • Hitler promoted Goebbels to *Gauleiter* of Berlin as a reward for supporting him. • The 'socialist' principles of the Nazi Party were weakened. • Hitler now had the freedom to introduce any policies he liked.

Reasons for limited support, 1923–29

By 1929, the Nazi Party was well organised. It had 100,000 members and Hitler had strong control over the party. However, in some ways, these were difficult years, where the Nazis had limited support. There were several reasons for this.

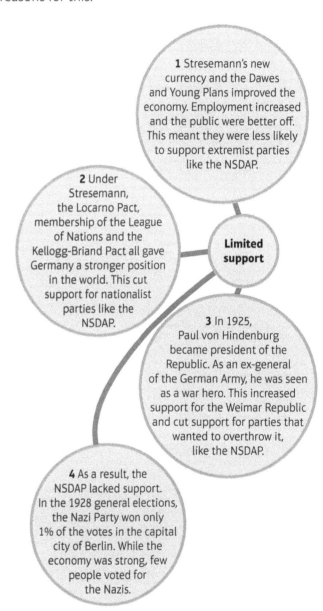

Figure 2.3 Reasons for limited Nazi support, 1923–29.

Source J

A confidential report on the Nazis by the Interior Ministry, July 1927.

```
A numerically insignificant... radical-
revolutionary splinter group incapable of
exerting any noticeable influence on the
great mass of the people and the course of
political events.
```

As a result, moderate parties did well between 1924 and 1928, and all the extreme parties lost support. In the general elections of May 1928, the Nazis:

- won only 12 seats
- were only the seventh biggest Reichstag party
- received only 810,000 votes – just 2.6% of the total vote.

Activities ?

1 a Create a table with two columns entitled:

- How Hitler's reorganisation made the Nazi Party more effective.
- How Hitler's reorganisation increased his own control.

b Do you think the reorganisation did more good for the party as a whole, or for Hitler's individual power? Debate this in a group, then write your own opinion.

2 a List the reasons why, despite all Hitler's work, the Nazis were still relatively weak in 1928 (see Figure 2.3 on page 57).

b Identify which of these was the main reason and explain your choice.

Summary

- Hitler launched the Munich Putsch in November 1923, in an attempt to take control of Germany.
- The Munich Putsch failed, but in some ways Hitler and the Nazis benefited.
- Hitler relaunched the Nazi Party in 1925, having set out his ideas in *Mein Kampf*.
- Hitler reformed the central and national organisation of the Nazi Party.
- Hitler strengthened his control over the party and over the SA.
- By 1928, the Nazis had little influence in the Reichstag.

Checkpoint

Strengthen

S1 Describe the events of the Munich Putsch.

S2 Explain Hitler's political views, as he wrote about them in *Mein Kampf*.

S3 Describe how Hitler improved the central and national organisation of his party.

S4 Give details of how strong the Nazi Party was by 1928, by considering the support they had and how organised they were, including the strength and impact of the SA.

Challenge

C1 Why did Hitler launch the Munich Putsch in 1923?

How confident do you feel about your answers to these questions? If you are unsure, look again at pages 49–57 for S1–S4; for C1, you could join together with others and discuss a joint answer. Your teacher can provide hints.

Learning outcomes

- Understand the reasons for the growth of Nazi support, including the consequences of the Wall Street Crash and the appeal of Hitler and the SA.

Why, in just a few months, did people's confidence in the Weimar Republic disappear?

- On 3 October 1929, Stresemann died. This was a severe blow to the Weimar Republic.
- Later in October 1929, there was a world economic crisis, known as the **Great Depression**. In Germany, it caused major economic problems, massive unemployment and a political crisis.

The Wall Street Crash in the USA

In October 1929, share* prices began to fall rapidly on the Wall Street stock exchange* in New York, USA. This meant that the value of many people's investments* fell hugely. Within a week, investors had lost $4,000 million.

This event is known as the Wall Street Crash.

Economic effects in Germany

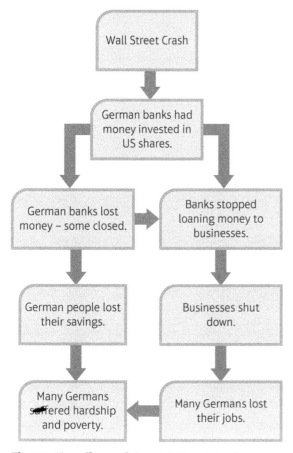

Figure: The effects of the Wall Street Crash on Germany.

People rushed to the banks to get their money out – causing some German banks to run out of cash.

The collapse of German banking then caused a general economic collapse in German industry. To pay out the money demanded by their account holders, German and American banks began to demand the return of money they had lent to businesses. Without this money, German industries and farms had to cut back production or even close down completely. The economy collapsed.

Source A

A photograph of people crowding outside the locked doors of the German Civil Servant Bank in 1929, demanding their money back.

Key terms

Shares*

When people invest their money in companies and businesses.

Stock exchange*

A place where shares are bought and sold.

Investment*

To put your money into shares.

Unemployment

The crisis resulted in very high unemployment.

- When the banks demanded their money back from German industries and farms, they had to reduce production or close. Either way, workers lost their jobs.
- The economic crisis was worldwide. German companies that sold their goods abroad found that their sales fell. More workers lost their jobs.
- German workers who were unemployed became poorer. They couldn't afford to buy as much. This meant that sales fell even further and companies had to make even more workers unemployed.

Years	Fall in industrial output*
1929–30	10% fall
1929–31	30% fall
1929–32	40% fall

Key terms

Industrial output*

The amount of industrial goods, like iron and steel, produced by a country.

Shanty town*

An area of poor-quality, makeshift houses.

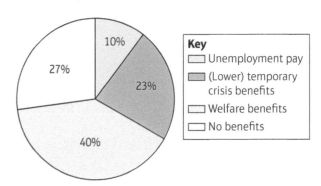

Figure 2.4 How the unemployed were helped financially by the government. 27% received no benefits.

Unemployment – the impact on people

Unemployment
- In September 1929, 1.3 million people were unemployed. By January 1933, this had risen to 6.1 million unemployed.
- Half of 16–30-year-olds were unemployed.
- The government had to cut unemployment benefits.

The impact of the Great Depression on people

Crime
- Crime rose as people were desperate.
- There was a 24% increase in arrests for theft in Berlin.

Savers
- The value of savings decreased.
- Some people lost all they had saved.

Homelessness
- People could not afford their rent or mortgage. They became homeless.
- Shanty towns* made up of shacks developed.

Workers
- Taxes increased to cover the cost of benefits.
- Between 1928 and 1932, wages fell by 30%.

Figure: Effects of the Great Depression

Activities

1 Look at the flow diagram on page 59. Write two or three sentences explaining how one event led to the next.

2 Write a sentence or two to explain how **economic collapse (1929–32)** might lead to people wanting political change.

The failure to deal with unemployment

People demanded political action, but the Weimar government failed them. From 1930 to 1932, the chancellor was Heinrich Brüning, leader of the Centre Party.

- He suggested increasing taxes to pay for unemployment benefits.
- He also reduced the amount of time for which people could claim benefits.

This pleased no one.

- Right-wing parties and the wealthy were against paying higher taxes.
- Left-wing parties and the workers were unhappy that unemployment benefit would be reduced.
- The politicians in the Reichstag could not agree on what should be done.

Brüning had lost control of the Reichstag, the economy and the streets. He resigned in May 1932.

Rise in support for KPD and NSDAP

As life became harder, people switched from the moderate political parties and to supporting extremist parties such as the Nazi Party (NSDAP) and the Communist Party (KPD).

General elections, 1928–32: seats in the Reichstag			
	May 1928	Sept 1930	July 1932
Social Democrats (SPD)	152	143	133
Nazi Party (NSDAP)	12	107	230
Communists (KPD)	54	77	89

Growing support for the Communist Party (KPD)

As Germany's social and economic problems increased during the Great Depression, support for the German Communist Party (KPD) grew. Whereas 10% of voters supported the KPD in the Reichstag elections of 1928, 15% of voters supported them in 1932.

Figure: The unpopularity of the Weimar Republic led to growing support for the Communist Party and the Nazi Party. Working-class people supported the KPD, wealthier people and businessmen supported the NSDAP.

Why did people support the Nazi Party?

The growth in support for the Nazis from 1929 to 1933 was huge. Why did it happen?

The appeal of Hitler and the SA

Many Germans were fed up with the Weimar Republic. They thought its government was weak, and that it had failed to solve economic problems. They saw Hitler and the Nazis as an alternative.

In Hitler, they saw a strong leader who promised:

- to restore law and order
- to force other countries to scrap the Treaty of Versailles and treat Germany fairly.

Hitler was very popular.

- He appeared on posters.
- He travelled around the country making speeches.
- He used aeroplanes to get around quickly.
- Wealthy business people funded the Nazi Party.

The SA was another reason why Germans supported the Nazi Party.

- The uniformed SA made the Nazis seem organised, disciplined and reliable. During the economic crisis, the SA made the Nazis look strong enough to control unrest.
- The SA were also used to disrupt opposition parties. The Nazis had a stronger private army than the communists. The elections of 1930 and 1932 were violent. Armed SA intimidated their opposition's supporters, and disrupted their meetings.

The appeal of the Nazis to different sections of German society

The Nazis also had particular policies that appealed to different groups in German society (Interpretation 1).

Source B

From an interview with a member of the Nazi Party.

... for five years I remained unemployed and I was broken both in body and spirit and I learned how stupid were all my dreams in those hard days at university. I was not wanted by Germany... then I was introduced to Hitler. You won't understand and I cannot explain either because I don't know what happened, but life for me took on a tremendous new significance... I committed myself, body, soul and spirit, to the movement.

Interpretation 1

From *The Coming of the Third Reich*, by Richard J. Evans, published in 2004.

... Nazi propaganda... skilfully targeted specific groups in the German electorate*... providing topics for particular venues and picking the speaker to fit the occasion. The... Party recognised the growing divisions of German society into competing interest groups in the course of the Depression and tailored their message to their particular constituency. The Nazis adapted... a whole range of posters and leaflets designed to win over different parts of the electorate.

Big business

- Targeted by the Nazi Party due to their wealth.
- Hitler said that the Nazi Party would protect big business from the rise of the communists.
- Wealthy businessmen, like Benz and Krupp, gave money to the party.

Working-class support

- The Nazi Party tried to seem like the party for the working classes. The Nazis supported traditional German values which were popular with many workers.
- The Nazis promised people 'work and bread'.
- However, more workers preferred the communists.

Middle-class* support

- The middle classes often owned businesses and/or had savings.
- Many had lost their savings in the Great Depression.
- They saw Hitler as a strong leader who could help Germany recover.

Farmers

- Many farmers hoped that Hitler would protect them from the Communist Party, which wanted to take their land.
- In the 1930 elections, the Nazis gained 60% of the votes in some rural areas.

Young people

- The Nazis targeted support from young Germans.
- For some young people, the Nazi Party was exciting. Nazi meetings were lively and interesting.
- Hitler's speeches were exciting and inspiring to some young people.

Women

- At first, many women did not support the Nazis.
- The Nazis said that women should play a traditional role in society as wives and mothers.
- Nazi propaganda said that voting for the Nazi Party was best for their families. Increasingly, many women came to see this as attractive.

Figure: How Nazi Party policies appealed to different groups.

Interpretation 2

From *The Weimar Republic*, by John Hiden, published in 1996.

More than any other party, the NSDAP depended on the crisis for its successful growth. The official membership statistics show an increase from 129,000 to 849,000 from 1930 to 1933…

No fewer than 43% of new members entering the party… were aged 18–30…

The preponderance [number] of petit-bourgeoisie [lower middle class] was particularly striking. White-collar workers [office workers], artisans [skilled craftsmen], merchants, shopkeepers and civil servants were twice as strongly represented in the NSDAP than in society as a whole. Manual workers were under-represented (but) of the 270,000 workers who did join the party, 150,000 were unemployed.

Key terms

Electorate*	Middle-class*
People with the right to vote.	Professional people, such as teachers and lawyers, as well as owners of small businesses.

Source C

A Nazi Party poster from 1932, appealing to women to support Adolf Hitler for the sake of their family.

Unity – something for everyone

The Nazis targeted support from different groups in society. But the Nazi appeal was not just to groups. They called for the **whole nation** to unite (see Source D). Some historians say this was new for German politics and helped the NSDAP to grow, as shown in Interpretation 3.

Source D

Hitler's speech to the people of Germany on the day of his appointment as Chancellor of Germany on 31 January 1933.

We do not recognise classes. The German people, with its millions of farmers, citizens and workers, will, together, overcome distress*.

Interpretation 3

From *Adolf Hitler*, by John Toland, published in 1976.

In 1930, he was offering something new to Germans – unity. He welcomed all. There was no class distinction*; the only demand was to follow him in his fight against Jews and Reds [communists], in his struggle for Lebensraum* and the glory and good of Germany.

Activities ?

1 What evidence is there on pages 61–64 that the Nazi Party grew in popularity, 1929–33?

2 Divide your class into groups representing big business, farmers, the working class, the middle class, young Germans and women. Each group should try to explain why some people within their group would have supported the Nazis.

   a Write two or three sentences arguing which group you think was most important, and why.

   b Write two or three sentences arguing which group you think was least important, and why.

Key terms

Distress*

Hardship.

Class distinction*

Treating people differently depending upon their economic backgrounds and wealth.

Lebensraum*

'Living space'. The Nazis believed that the German people needed more land on which to live.

THINKING HISTORICALLY Interpretations (2c/3a)

History as hypotheses

In science, you might have come across the idea of a hypothesis – a hypothesis is an idea that a scientist comes up with to explain what they can see happening. The scientist then tries to find evidence, through experiments, to find out whether their hypothesis is correct. Historians often work in a similar way, but look at sources to find their evidence, rather than doing experiments.

These three historians are thinking about the reasons for the rise of the Nazi Party.

Historian's interests	Historian's hypothesis	Evidence
Political historian: Interested in relationships between nations and political leaders, their views and actions and the effects these had on history.		
Economic historian: Interested in how the economy changed, and how this affected groups in society and their political views.		
Cultural historian: Interested in the ideas in society, how these ideas change and how these ideas affect what people do.	The main reasons for the rise of the Nazi Party were ideas like nationalism. Hitler used these to come to power.	'Many German nationalists felt that their country had been disgraced after the First World War, and so supported Hitler who promised to make Germany great again.'

Work in groups of three.

1   Make a copy of the above table.

   a   As a group, discuss the interests of each historian and write a hypothesis that they might put forward based on their interests (the cultural historian has been done for you).

   b   Each person in the group should take on the role of one of the historians. For your historian, add at least three pieces of evidence into the table that support your hypothesis, based on the information and sources in this chapter.

   c   For your historian, write a final paragraph, summing up your views on the reasons for the rise of the Nazi Party. Write your hypothesis first and then support it with evidence.

2   Share your concluding paragraphs with the rest of the group and compare them.

   Look at each hypothesis in turn. Can you think of at least one piece of evidence that challenges each hypothesis? (Tip: you can start by looking at evidence for the other hypotheses being right!)

3   Discuss as a group: Is it possible to say which hypothesis is correct?

Exam-style question, Section B

Study Interpretation 1 (page 62) and Interpretation 3 (page 64). They give different views about the reasons for the appeal of the Nazi Party to the German people, 1929–33.

What is the main difference between these views?

Explain your answer, using details from both interpretations.   **4 marks**

Exam tip

It is not enough just to find differences of detail between the interpretations.

The key is:

- to begin by identifying what the **view** of each interpretation is. For example, you might write, 'Interpretation 1 gives the view that the appeal of the Nazi Party was because of…'
- to decide how the **view** in one interpretation is different from the other
- to **use the detail** in each interpretation to show how the views differ. Take quotes from the interpretation that you can use to support your statement about what the view of the interpretation is.

Summary

- By the start of 1929, the Nazi Party had little political power in Germany.
- However, by 1932, the Nazi Party had 230 seats in the German Reichstag.
- A key factor in the rise of the Nazi Party was the economic crisis caused by the Wall Street Crash.
- The economic crisis included a banking collapse, a fall in industrial output, rising unemployment and falling wages.
- The Weimar government failed to solve these problems.
- As a result, support grew for extremist parties like the Communist Party and the Nazi Party.
- Support for the Nazis came from several different groups in German society.

Checkpoint

Strengthen

S1 Describe the events of the Wall Street Crash.

S2 Explain the impact of the Wall Street Crash on Germany.

S3 Describe how the German chancellor, Brüning, tried to solve the economic crisis.

S4 Describe the effect of the economic crisis on support for the Nazi Party.

S5 Describe which sections of German society supported the Nazi Party.

Challenge

C1 Explain how the appeal of the Nazi Party was attractive to German society as a whole.

How confident do you feel about your answers to these questions? If you are unsure, look again at pages 59–64 for S1–S6; for C1, you could join together with others and discuss a joint answer. Your teacher can provide hints.

2.4 How Hitler became Chancellor, 1932–33

Learning outcomes

- Examine how Hitler became Chancellor, and understand why it happened.

As 1932 began, the Weimar Republic was suffering from many economic problems. The chancellor and leader of the Centre Party, Heinrich Brüning, was struggling to make the Weimar Republic work.

However, Hitler was far from coming to power.

- In the general elections of 1930, the Nazi Party had won only 107 seats out of 577 in the Reichstag.

- The Nazis had only received 18% of the votes in the election. The moderate Social Democratic Party had 25%.

Despite this, within a year, in January 1933, Hitler became Chancellor. How did this happen?

Figure 2.5 gives the outline of events.

Source A

A painting showing a lorry full of Nazi SA stormtroopers driving through a working-class area outside KPD headquarters.

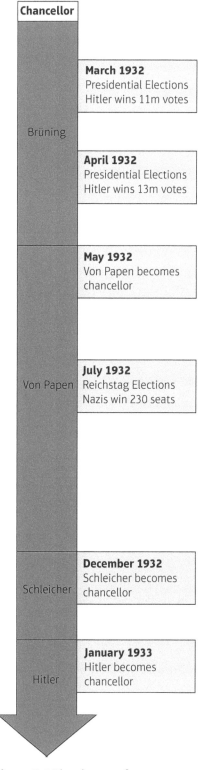

Chancellor	
Brüning	**March 1932** Presidential Elections Hitler wins 11m votes
	April 1932 Presidential Elections Hitler wins 13m votes
Von Papen	**May 1932** Von Papen becomes chancellor
	July 1932 Reichstag Elections Nazis win 230 seats
Schleicher	**December 1932** Schleicher becomes chancellor
Hitler	**January 1933** Hitler becomes chancellor

Figure 2.5 The change of governments, 1932–33.

Political developments in 1932

March 1932: Hindenburg stands for re-election

Hindenburg's term as President ended in 1932. By this time, he was 84 and very weak, but he was persuaded to stand for election again, to keep the government stable. When the election took place, in March 1932, the results were as follows.

Ernst Thälmann, leader of the KPD	Hindenburg	Adolf Hitler, leader of the NSDAP
5 million votes (14%)	18 million votes (49.6%)	11 million votes (30%)

April 1932: Hindenburg stands for re-election again

Because no candidate achieved 50% of the vote, the election was repeated in April.

- Hitler campaigned hard.
- He rented an aeroplane and flew from town to town making speeches.
- The SA disrupted communist meetings and fought in the streets with Hitler's political opponents.

Hindenburg was re-elected, but the results were good for Hitler.

Ernst Thälmann	Hindenburg	Adolf Hitler
4 million votes (11%)	19 million votes (53%)	13 million votes (36%)

30 May 1932: Chancellor Brüning resigns

However, Hindenburg's re-election did not bring stability. In April 1932, the moderate Chancellor, Heinrich Brüning, took two steps which lost him widespread support in the Reichstag.

- He banned the SA and SS in order to calm unrest and to control the Nazis.
- He announced a plan to buy up land and use it to house the unemployed.

Source B

A campaign poster in the presidential elections of 1932. It says that Germany would be on the road to self-destruction unless Hindenburg was re-elected.

These measures united the right-wing groups against Brüning.

- The ban on the SA and SS angered Hitler.
- Landowners, including President Hindenburg, were furious about the plan to buy up their land.

Brüning lost the support of the President and the majority of the Reichstag. He was unable to govern and resigned on 30 May 1932.

Von Schleicher suggests a new Chancellor

An important army general called Kurt von Schleicher encouraged right-wing parties to join together. To lead this coalition, he chose a wealthy politician called Franz von Papen.

Hitler and the Nazis agreed to support Schleicher's coalition if the ban on the SA was lifted.

Schleicher encouraged President Hindenburg to ignore the Reichstag and to rule using decrees.* This was so undemocratic that the new government was known as 'the Cabinet of Barons' (see Interpretation 1).

If we work together we can take control of the government and sort out the country.

We shall get Hindenburg to make me chancellor.

Von Schleicher   **Von Papen**

Interpretation 1

From *The Coming of the Third Reich*, by Richard J. Evans, published in 2004.

These events marked… the end of parliamentary democracy in Germany. Papen and Schleicher saw themselves as creating a 'New State', above parties, indeed opposed to a multi-party system.

30 May 1932: von Papen becomes Chancellor

On 30 May 1932, Hindenburg made von Papen Chancellor.

July 1932: Reichstag elections

Von Papen's new government was in trouble from the start.

In July 1932, there were elections for the Reichstag. Once again, this caused violence in the streets, between the armed private armies of the Nazi Party and the Communist Party (see Source C).

Source C

From *Berlin Stories*, by Christopher Isherwood, published in 1945. Isherwood was a British journalist living in Berlin at the time Hitler came to power in Germany.

Each week there were new emergency decrees. Brüning's weary episcopal [priest-like] voice issued commands...and was not obeyed... Berlin was in a state of civil war. Hate exploded...out of nowhere; at street corners, in restaurants, cinemas … at midnight … in the middle of the afternoon. Knives were whipped out, blows were dealt with spiked rings … chair-legs, or leaded clubs; bullets slashed the advertisements... In the middle of a crowded street a young man would be attacked... thrashed, and left bleeding on the pavement. "[Bruning] is weak" [they] said. "What these swine need is a man with hair on his chest." … People said that the Nazis would be in power by Christmas.

When the results were announced, the NSDAP had won 230 seats in the Reichstag. This was a great result for the Nazis. Hitler demanded that Hindenburg sack von Papen and appoint him as Chancellor instead.

We are the most popular party, you must make me chancellor.

I do not want an extremist like Hitler in power.

Hitler   **Hindenburg**

November 1932: von Papen is sacked

Hindenburg refused to make Hitler Chancellor. Instead, von Papen called new Reichstag elections, hoping that Nazi support would fall.

Nazi seats in the Reichstag did fall, but they were still the largest party.

At this point, von Schleicher abandoned von Papen. He persuaded Hindenburg to force von Papen to resign.

Key term

Decrees*
Laws introduced by the president without the support of the Reichstag.

December 1932: von Schleicher becomes Chancellor

Hindenburg was, by now, struggling to find a strong government. But he still refused to make Hitler Chancellor. He appointed von Schleicher as Chancellor instead.

January 1933: Hitler becomes Chancellor

Von Schleicher's chancellorship had no real support. With Hitler and the Nazis now against him, von Schleicher was unable to govern. Von Schleicher asked Hindenburg to make him head of a military dictatorship*.

Source D

A 1933 cartoon from the British political magazine *Punch*. It shows Hindenburg (on the left) and von Papen (on the right) lifting Hitler to power.

THE TEMPORARY TRIANGLE.

Von Hindenburg and Von Papen (*together*)—
"FOR HE'S A JOLLY GOOD FELLOW,
FOR HE'S A JOLLY GOOD FELLOW,
FOR HE'S A JOLLY GOOD FE-EL-LOW,
(*Aside:* "Confound him!")
AND SO SAY BOTH OF US!"

Hindenburg refused.

Rumours began to spread that Schleicher was going to take power with force, using the army. Von Papen suggested a solution to Hindenburg: make Hitler the Chancellor and von Papen the Vice Chancellor. This way, Hindenburg and von Papen thought they could make all the decisions themselves and just use Hitler for his popularity, but give him little power. The president agreed. As a result, on 30 January 1933, Adolf Hitler became the Chancellor of Germany.

The roles of Hindenburg, von Schleicher and von Papen

Hitler's rise to Chancellor was caused by a range of factors, including Hitler's appeal, the policies and organisation of the Nazi Party, the economic collapse of 1929–33 and the weaknesses of the Weimar Republic. But Hindenburg, von Schleicher and von Papen also had their roles.

- **Hindenburg** never fully supported the Weimar Republic and democratic government. He was happy to govern without the Reichstag, which weakened it.
- **Von Schleicher and von Papen** both wanted to move away from government by the Reichstag and towards a 'stronger' government controlled by wealthy people. Their plots to increase their own power undermined the Weimar Republic.
- **All three** misjudged Hitler. They all believed they could control Hitler and the Nazis. They were wrong.

Key term

Dictatorship*

Government by a single ruler who has complete power.

Activities ?

1. Draw your own timeline, from January 1932 to January 1933. Mark on it all the key events that led to the appointment of Adolf Hitler as Chancellor of Germany.

2. Make a five-column table with the following headings: Brüning (see page 68), Hitler, Hindenberg, von Schleicher, von Papen (all on pages 69 and 70). Look through the events of 1932–33, then:

   a. Jot down details in each column every time one of the key people does anything that eventually leads to Hitler's appointment as Chancellor.

   b. Write two or three sentences to summarise who you think was most responsible.

THINKING HISTORICALLY Interpretations (4b)

Historical method is everything: what does good historical writing look like?

Bad history		Good history
Based on gut feeling	⟷	Based on considering the evidence
Poor historical argument – points do not link together	⟷	Good historical argument – points link together
No supporting evidence	⟷	Evidence used to support argument

Conclusion 1

I think that Hitler becoming Chancellor was a disaster. He had wild policies but people just fell under his spell. So they voted for him. By 1933 he had so many supporters that he forced himself upon the country and became Chancellor. Hindenburg, von Schleicher and von Papen were fools. But they had no alternative. Hitler made them make him Chancellor.

Conclusion 2

Hitler became Chancellor in 1933 because of the economic depression. Because they were suffering from unemployment and poverty, people voted for extreme parties like the Nazi Party and the Communist Party. So Hitler became stronger. We can see this from his election results. He did not force himself on the country. But, by 1933, Hindenburg was desperate because von Papen told him there would be a rebellion if he did not appoint Hitler as Chancellor.

Conclusion 3

Many factors resulted in Hitler's appointment as Chancellor in 1933. One factor was the economic situation. Unemployment reached six million. This increased poverty, and people, in their desperation, voted for extreme parties. By 1932, the Nazi Party

had 230 seats in the Reichstag. As leader of the biggest party, Hitler had a good case to be Chancellor. But another factor was the mistakes made by Hindenburg, von Schleicher and von Papen. None of them really wanted a democracy. They hoped to create a 'New State' run by the wealthy. They thought that, if they included Hitler in their new government, the people of Germany would accept it. They thought they could control Hitler. They were wrong.

Work in pairs. Read the above conclusions and answer the questions.

1. Look at all the conclusions. In what ways do they differ from one another?

2. Look carefully at the table above.

   a. Where would you place each student's conclusion on the line between 'Bad history' and 'Good history'? Are they examples of 'bad history', 'good history', or somewhere in between? Explain your answer.

   b. Suggest one improvement to each conclusion to move it towards 'good' historical writing.

Exam-style question, Section B

Study Source B (page 68) and Source C (page 69).

How useful are Sources B and C for an enquiry into the strength of democracy in Germany by 1932?

Explain your answer, using Sources B and C and your knowledge of the historical context.   **8 marks**

Exam tip

A good answer will consider:

- how useful the information in each source is for this particular enquiry. To do this, you will need to consider what the sources suggest about how strong democracy was in Germany by 1932.
- how the provenance (i.e. the type of source, its origin, author or purpose) of each source affects how useful it is. If we cannot trust the author of the source to give an accurate account, then that might make the source less useful.
- how knowledge of the historical context affects a judgement of how useful each source is. Does what you know about Germany in 1932 agree with the source? If so, then that suggests it is more reliable, and more useful.

Summary

- At the start of 1932, Hitler had little political power.
- However, in January 1933, he was appointed Chancellor of the Weimar Republic.
- One reason was Hitler's success in the presidential elections of 1932.
- Another reason was the success of the Nazi Party in the Reichstag elections of 1932.
- A further reason was that politicians such as von Schleicher and von Papen plotted to remove Chancellor Brüning and reduce the power of the Reichstag.
- Von Schleicher and von Papen both thought that they could include Hitler and the Nazis in their governments and then control them.
- There was a general fear that civil war might break out if Germany could not find a strong government with widespread popular support.
- President Hindenburg did not want Hitler to be Chancellor, but finally agreed.

Checkpoint

Strengthen

S1 Describe the events of the presidential elections of March and April 1932.

S2 Describe how Brüning lost his position as German Chancellor.

S3 Describe how von Papen came to power as German Chancellor.

S4 Describe the results of the Reichstag elections of July 1932.

S5 Describe how von Papen was replaced by von Schleicher in December 1932.

S6 Describe how von Schleicher was replaced by Hitler in January 1933.

Challenge

C1 Identify the factors that helped Hitler become Chancellor in 1933.

How confident do you feel about your answers to these questions? If you are unsure, look again at pages 67–70 for S1–S6; for C1, you could join together with others and discuss a joint answer. Your teacher can provide hints.

Recap: Hitler's rise to power, 1919–33

Recall quiz

1 What was the full (English) name of the DAP?
2 What was the full (English) name of the NSDAP?
3 What was *Der Stürmer*?
4 What was Hitler's *Stosstrupp*?
5 What is the meaning of the word *Putsch* in Munich Putsch?
6 Who was elected as the German president in 1925?
7 Who was the German Chancellor from 1930 to 1932?
8 Who was the German Chancellor from May to November 1932?
9 Who became the German Chancellor in December 1932?
10 Who became the German Chancellor in January 1933?

Activities ?

1 In February 1920, Hitler and the DAP produced the Twenty-Five Point Programme. Page 43 lists nine of these points. List as many as you can.

2 Hitler attracted supporters to the DAP because of his appeal as a speaker. List three things that made him a good public speaker (see page 44).

3 Hitler improved the organisation of the DAP. Complete the following sentences that explain some of the ways he did this.
   a The new name for the DAP was…
   b The swastika and the straight arm salute were…
   c The *Völkischer Beobachter* was…

4 Who was Ernst Röhm?

5 Make a list of three things that you know about the SA (*Sturmabteilung*).

6 In one sentence each, give one long-term, one medium-term and one short-term cause of the Munich Putsch of 1923.

7 Make a timeline of the events of the Munich Putsch from the evening of 8 November to the end of 9 November 1923.

8 List two reasons why the Munich Putsch could be seen as a failure and two reasons why it could be seen as a success.

9 Briefly describe these features of Hitler's beliefs, as described in *Mein Kampf*:
   a nationalism
   b socialism
   c traditional German values.

10 Briefly describe these features of the Nazi Party after 1924:
   a party headquarters and national organisation
   b SS (*Schutzstaffel*)
   c Bamberg Conference, 1926.

11 'The Nazi Party had achieved very limited success by the end of 1928.' Give two facts that support this statement.

12 Briefly explain to a friend what the Great Depression of 1929 was and how it affected Germany.

13 Support for the Nazi Party increased, 1929–33. Explain its appeal to the following groups:
   a the owners of big businesses
   b the working class
   c the middle class
   d farmers
   e young people
   f women.

14 Sketch a timeline of events from January 1932 to January 1933 to show how Hitler became Chancellor of the Weimar Republic.

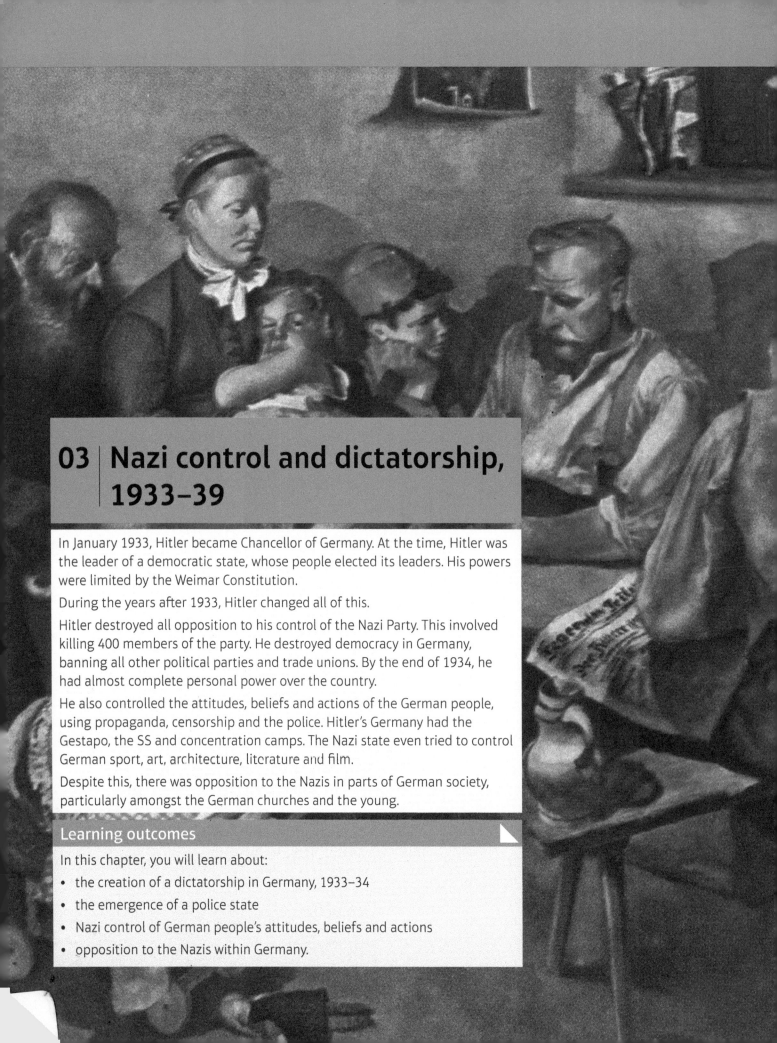

03 | Nazi control and dictatorship, 1933–39

In January 1933, Hitler became Chancellor of Germany. At the time, Hitler was the leader of a democratic state, whose people elected its leaders. His powers were limited by the Weimar Constitution.

During the years after 1933, Hitler changed all of this.

Hitler destroyed all opposition to his control of the Nazi Party. This involved killing 400 members of the party. He destroyed democracy in Germany, banning all other political parties and trade unions. By the end of 1934, he had almost complete personal power over the country.

He also controlled the attitudes, beliefs and actions of the German people, using propaganda, censorship and the police. Hitler's Germany had the Gestapo, the SS and concentration camps. The Nazi state even tried to control German sport, art, architecture, literature and film.

Despite this, there was opposition to the Nazis in parts of German society, particularly amongst the German churches and the young.

Learning outcomes

In this chapter, you will learn about:

- the creation of a dictatorship in Germany, 1933–34
- the emergence of a police state
- Nazi control of German people's attitudes, beliefs and actions
- opposition to the Nazis within Germany.

3.1 The creation of a dictatorship, 1933–34

Learning outcomes

- Understand the events surrounding the Reichstag fire, and the significance of it.
- Understand how Hitler gained more power with the introduction of the Enabling Act, and his removal of opposition groups.
- Understand the events surrounding the Night of the Long Knives.

From 30 January 1933, Hitler was Chancellor of Germany. But his power was limited.

- The Weimar Constitution limited what the Chancellor could do.
- Hindenburg had all the powers of the President.
- Hitler's cabinet* had 12 members – but only two were NSDAP* members.
- Only about one-third of the Reichstag* were NSDAP.

Most people thought other politicians would control Hitler. But they were wrong. Hitler was looking for a chance to increase his own power. He used a fire at the Reichstag to help him do so.

The Reichstag Fire

On 27 February 1933, the Reichstag building burned down in a huge fire.

A Dutch communist named Marinus van der Lubbe was caught on the site with matches and firelighters. He said he started the fire and was put on trial. He was found guilty and executed.

However, Hitler claimed that van der Lubbe was part of a major communist plot against the government. The Nazis used the Reichstag Fire as an opportunity to attack the communists.

Key terms

Cabinet*

A group of the most senior members of a government.

NSDAP*

The initials for the official name of the Nazi Party.

Reichstag*

The German parliament.

Joseph Goebbels*

A leading Nazi who later became Minister of Propaganda for the Party.

Source A

From the memoirs (like a diary but one that is written from memory after the time) of Rudolf Diels, Head of the Prussian Police, published in 1950. Diels was in charge of questioning van der Lubbe. Here he is recalling Hitler's reaction to the Reichstag Fire in 1933.

Hitler... started screaming at the top of his voice. 'Now we'll show them! The German people have been soft too long. Every Communist official must be shot. All Communist deputies must be hanged tonight. All friends of the Communists must be locked up. And that goes for the Social Democrats too.'

Source B

A cartoon from the German magazine *Kladderdatsch* in 1933. *Kladdertatsch* was a satirical magazine which put forward strong opinions on political events. This illustration shows Joseph Goebbels*, pulling evidence of a communist plot out of a box.

Source C

A photograph taken inside the Reichstag soon after the Reichstag Fire.

The Reichstag Fire had a number of important consequences that helped Hitler and the Nazis to increase their power.

THINKING HISTORICALLY **Thinking Historically – Evidence (3b)**

It depends on the question

When considering the usefulness of a historical source, people often look at whether a witness can be trusted. In other words, is the source reliable? This is important. However, some sources are not witnesses – they are simply the remains of the past.

Work in small groups.

1   Imagine you are investigating the impact of the Reichstag Fire on politics in Germany.

   a   Write two statements that you could make about the impact of the Reichstag Fire on politics in Germany based on Source C.

   b   Which of your statements are you most sure of? Explain your answer.

2   Source B is an unreliable account – it is a political cartoon which gives a one-sided view of events. Try to think of at least two statements that you can still reasonably make about the impact of the Reichstag Fire on politics in Germany, using this source.

3   Which source is more useful for investigating the impact of the Reichstag Fire on politics in Germany? Explain your answer in two or three sentences.

4   In your group, discuss the following question. Just because a source is unreliable, does that mean it is of no use to a historian?

Key term

Decree*

An official order that has the same power as a law.

Consequence of the Reichstag Fire	How this helped Hitler and the Nazis
Four thousand communists were arrested on the night of the fire.	As the communists were the enemies of the Nazis, this weakened their opposition.
Hitler told President Hindenburg that the communists were trying to take over the government. To stop them, Hitler got Hindenburg to declare a state of national emergency.	This gave Hitler the power to make decrees*, even without the support of the Reichstag.
Hitler issued the Decree for the Protection of the People and the State.	This gave him the power to arrest political opponents, and to shut down the newspapers of other parties.
Hitler banned all Communist Party members from the Reichstag.	This meant the NSDAP had fewer opponents in the Reichstag.
Hindenburg announced a new election to take place in March 1933.	The NSDAP did very well in the election, and increased its Reichstag members to 288. This meant that the Nazis now had the majority of support in the Reichstag, so they could pass new laws.

The Enabling Act

In March 1933, Hitler asked the Reichstag to pass the Enabling Act*. He wanted to destroy the power of the Reichstag. The Enabling Act would help him to do this. Nazi Party stormtroopers* were used to frighten anyone who tried to oppose Hitler (see Source E).

The Enabling Act said that:

- the Reich Cabinet* could pass new laws
- these laws could overrule the constitution of the Weimar Republic
- the laws would be put forward by the Chancellor – Hitler.

The Enabling Act would give Hitler the right to make laws for four years without the support of the Reichstag.

Source E

From *Knaves, Fools and Heroes* by Sir John Wheeler-Bennet, published in 1974. Wheeler-Bennet lived in Germany in 1934. Here, he is recalling the debate on the Enabling Act.

There were nearly 300 Nazi deputies and 50 or so Nationalist. There was a marked absence of Communists. There were fewer Social Democrats than could have been present, because some were in hospital, the victims of electoral violence; some had fled the country — and who could blame them?

Along the corridors, SS men, in their sinister black and silver uniforms, had been posted; their legs apart and arms crossed, their eyes fixed and cruel, looking like messengers of doom.

Outside, a mob of SA chanted threatening slogans: 'Give us the Bill or else fire and murder'. Their clamour [noise] was clearly audible within the chamber.

On 24 March 1933, without any communist members present, the Reichstag passed the Enabling Act by 444 votes to 94. Other Reichstag members who opposed the Nazis had been frightened into staying away.

The 1933 Enabling Act marked the end of democratic rule in Germany and the end of the Weimar Constitution and the Republic.

Key terms

Act*

A law.

Stormtrooper*

The name given to members of the SA, the private army of the Nazis.

Reich Cabinet*

The twelve leading ministers in the government, including Hitler and led by him.

Source D

From an official report by the SPD (Social Democratic Party) about the raid on their Braunschweig branch in March 1933.

The Nazis broke windows and came through the holes. They opened fire; the office marketing manager was shot in the stomach. Secretaries were driven with clubs and daggers and locked up for hours. The regular police blocked off the surrounding streets. The Nazis looted the building under their very eyes.

Removing other opposition

Once Hitler had the power to pass laws without the Reichstag, he set about removing other opponents.

Trade unions

Hitler believed that trade unions*, were being used to oppose the government (for example, workers could go on strike). Therefore, in May 1933:

- Nazis arrested trade union leaders
- Hitler banned trade unions and made strikes illegal.

Political parties

Hitler then began to remove all political opposition.

- In May 1933, Nazi stormtroopers went to the offices of the Social Democratic Party and the Communist Party, destroyed their newspapers and took all their money.
- In July 1933, Hitler issued a decree banning all political parties in Germany, except for the NSDAP (see Source F).

Source F

Law against the Establishment of Parties, 14 July 1933.

Article I The National Socialist German Workers' Party constitutes the only political party in Germany.

Article II Whoever undertakes to maintain the organisation of another political party or to form a new political party shall be punished with penal servitude* of up to three years or imprisonment of between six months and three years.

Key terms

Trade union*

An organised group of workers, acting together to protect their own interests.

Penal servitude*

Being sent to a labour camp where prisoners are forced to work, doing unpleasant jobs.

Liberties*

Freedoms and rights.

Source G

A British cartoon from July 1933, published in the *Daily Express*. It is showing President Hindenburg in the middle of a boxing ring holding up Hitler's hand in triumph. The defeated opponent in the corner is 'German Liberties*'.

Local government

Hitler controlled the central German government in Berlin. However, each area of Germany also had a local parliament, known as Länder parliaments. The Nazis did not control those.

So, in January 1934, Hitler shut down the Länder parliaments and appointed his supporters to run every region of Germany.

Activities ?

1 Here is a list of events which strengthened Hitler's control of Germany. Draw a timeline for 1933 and 1934 (you will complete it on page 81) and write on it the following events:

   a Hitler becomes Chancellor

   b The Reichstag Fire – Hindenburg calls a state of National Emergency

   c There is an election for new members of the Reichstag

   d The Enabling Act is passed

   e Trade unions are banned

   f All political parties are banned, except NSDAP

   g Länder parliaments are shut down.

2 Which of these events were legal and which were illegal? Illegal actions are when the rules and laws are not followed, for example, when violence is used. Discuss with a partner and mark your decisions on your timeline.

3 Between January 1933 and January 1934, was Hitler's power gained by legal or illegal means? Write three or four sentences to explain your view. You could start: 'I think Hitler gained power … because…'.

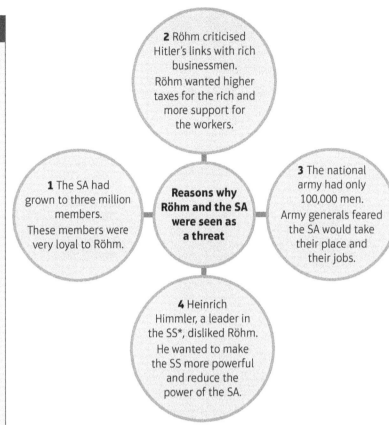

Figure: Why Hitler thought that Röhm could threaten his leadership.

The Night of the Long Knives

By the start of 1934, Hitler had made Germany a one-party state – the Nazi Party. He now made sure that no one could challenge him as the leader of the party.

Hitler believed that Ernst Röhm, the leader of the SA, (stormtroopers), was a threat to him.

Source H

From the book *Hitler Speaks*, published in 1940, by Hermann Rauschning, a Nazi official who emigrated from Germany in 1936. Here, he is quoting words spoken by Ernst Röhm, when he was drunk in 1934.

Adolf is a swine. His old friends are not good enough for him. Adolf is turning into a gentleman. He wants to sit on a hilltop and pretend he is God.

Hitler decided to remove the threat of Röhm and the SA. He arranged a meeting with Röhm and 100 other SA leaders on 30 June 1934. When they arrived, Röhm and the other senior officers of the SA were arrested, imprisoned and shot (see Source I). This event is known as **the Night of the Long Knives**.

Source I

Extracts from the diary of Alfred Rosenberg from 30 June 1934. Rosenberg was a leading Nazi.

With an SS escort, the Führer knocked gently on Roehm's [Röhm's] door: 'A message from Munich', he said in a disguised voice. 'Come in' Roehm shouted, 'the door is open'. Hitler tore open the door, fell on Roehm as he lay in bed, seized him by the throat and screamed, 'You are under arrest, you pig!' Then he turned him over to the SS.

Key term

SS*

The 'Schutzstaffel', or Protection Squad. They were Hitler's personal elite soldiers. See pages 83–84.

Interpretation 1

From *Life in Germany 1919–1945*, by Steve Waugh, published in 2009.

The greatest threat came from within the Nazi Party... Röhm, as leader of the SA, was a genuine threat to Hitler's own position as leader. Röhm was the commander of a very large organisation of men whose members were increasingly violent and out of control... Moreover, Röhm favoured a 'second revolution'... which would lead to more socialist policies. The purge* was also the result of a power struggle (between Röhm and) leading Nazis, like Herman Goering, the leader of the SS.

Interpretation 2

From *Germany 1918–45*, by G. Lacey and K. Shephard, published in 1971.

The smoothness with which the murders of 30 June were carried out is powerful proof that no Röhm plot was imminent [about to happen]. There was no resistance encountered anywhere. Many victims unsuspectingly surrendered voluntarily, believing it was a big mistake. The only shots fired were those of the executioners*.

Extend your knowledge

More murders

In addition to Röhm, about 400 people, including 150 senior members of the SA, were shot without trial. Leading politicians were also murdered. These included General von Schleicher – the ex-Chancellor.

The killing continues

During the Night of the Long Knives, von Papen (still Vice Chancellor), complained to Goering* about what was happening. In response to his complaints, the SS went to von Papen's office, shot one of his staff, and arrested the others. Von Papen's home was surrounded and his telephone cut off. It was now clear that he could not control Hitler.

Hitler was acting illegally, murdering his rivals for power.

Source J

A speech by Hitler in the Reichstag, on 13 July 1934.

```
I ordered the leaders of the guilty to be shot. If anyone
asks why I did not use the courts of justice, I say this:
in this hour, I was responsible for the fate of the German
people and I became the supreme judge of the German people.
```

Some Germans objected to the violence, but few knew how bad it was. They were pleased that the power of the SA, who were hated for their violence, had been cut back. The SA continued after 1934, but its power was limited. It was now under Hitler's control.

Key terms

Purge*

Getting rid of something or someone.

Executioner*

A person who puts someone to death.

Goering*

A leading Nazi who became one of the most powerful people in the Party.

Source K

Heinrich Himmler, head of the SS, at the front on the right, with Ernst Röhm, leader of the SA in 1933.

The death of Hindenburg

On 2 August 1934, President Hindenburg died. Hitler did two things to make sure he had total control of Germany:

• He announced that he was now Germany's Führer*. He said that, as Führer, he would add all of the President's powers to those he already held as Chancellor.

• He made every soldier in the army take an oath of loyalty* (or 'oath of allegiance') to him.

The Weimar Republic had formally ended. Hitler's Third Reich* had begun.

Activities

1 Complete the timeline which you started on page 79 by adding the following events:
   a The Night of the Long Knives
   b The death of Hindenburg
   c Hitler becomes Führer.

2 Discuss with a partner whether these were legal or illegal and mark this on your timeline.

3 a From February 1934 to August 1934, were Hitler's actions legal or illegal? Write two or three sentences to explain your answer.

   b Compare this answer with the answer which you wrote to the same question on page 79. Has anything changed?

Exam-style question, Section B

Study Interpretations 1 and 2 (page 80).

They give different views about the threat which Röhm posed to Hitler in 1934. What is the main difference between these views?

Explain your answer, using details from both interpretations.

4 marks

Exam tip

It is not enough just to find differences of detail between the interpretations.

The key is:

• to decide how the view in one interpretation is different from the other

• to use the detail in each interpretation to illustrate how the views differ.

Key terms

Führer*

German word for 'leader'. Hitler became known as the Führer from 1934.

Oath of loyalty*

A promise to support someone.

Third Reich*

Reich is a German word that means 'empire'. Hitler believed that before him there had been two great German empires in history. He wanted to build a third empire, a Third Reich.

Summary

- The Reichstag Fire allowed Hitler to begin creating a dictatorship* in Germany.
- After the fire, there were open attacks on communists and the Nazis gained more seats in the Reichstag.
- The Enabling Act changed Germany's constitution. It gave Hitler much more power. As Chancellor, he and his Reich Cabinet could pass laws without the support of the Reichstag.
- The Night of the Long Knives helped Hitler to take full control of the Nazi Party.
- After the death of Hindenburg, Hitler increased his power. On 19 August, the Weimar Republic formally ended.

Checkpoint

Strengthen

S1 Describe the events of the Reichstag Fire.

S2 What events led to the passing of the Enabling Act?

S3 Describe what the Enabling Act and laws limiting trade unions and political parties did.

S4 What was the Night of the Long Knives?

Challenge

C1 In what ways did Hitler have more power by the end of 1934 than in early 1933?

How confident do you feel about your answers to these questions? If you are unsure, look again at pages 75–80 for S1 to S4; for C1, discuss with others and consider a joint answer. Your teacher can provide hints.

Key term

Dictatorship*
When one person rules with total power and control.

3.2 The police state

- Understand the different parts of the Nazi police state*, including controlling Germany's legal and religious systems.
- Examine how far Hitler succeeded in creating a police state.

The German state which Hitler created after 1933 was a **police state**. The Nazi government used the police – often the secret police* – to control what people did and what they said. People who did or said anything bad about the Nazi Party were punished.

Hitler set up his own police and security forces. These were not run by the government. They were run by the Nazi Party and Hitler. Their role was to protect and support the Nazi Party.

Policing the police state

The main organisations used by Hitler to control this Nazi police state were the SS, the SD and the Gestapo (see Figure 3.1).

Key terms

Police state*

A government that uses the police and security forces to monitor and control the lives of ordinary people.

Secret police*

A police force that works in secret, spying on what people do.

Prosecute*

To try someone for an offence in a court of law.

Informant*

A person who gives information away. Informants would tell the Gestapo about people who they thought were opponents of the Nazis.

SS
(Protection Squad)
Heinrich Himmler
Black uniforms.
By 1936, the ss controlled all of Germany's police and security forces.

SD
(Security Service)
Reynhard Heydrich
Uniformed.
Spied on all known opponents and critics of the Nazi Party and the German government.

Gestapo
(Secret State Police)
Reynhard Heydrich
No uniforms.
Prosecuted* anyone who said or did anything against the Nazis or the government. Informants* gave the Gestapo information. Feared by the general public.

Figure 3.1 The structure of the Nazi police state.

The SS

Full name: *Schutzstaffel* or Protection Squad
Leader: Heinrich Himmler
Number of employees: 240,000
Their role:
- The main police force of the Nazi Party.
- In charge of all other police and security forces.

Other information:
- Himmler belived that the SS did not need to follow any laws (see Source A).
- Members of the SS were known as 'Blackshirts' due to the colour of their uniforms.
- SS members were carefully chosen. They had to fit what the Nazis believed to be perfect and pure Germans* (see Source B).

The SD

Full name: *Sicherheitsdienst* or Security Force
Leader: Reinhard Heydrich
Number of employees: Over 6,000 by 1944
Their role:
- To check on any opposition to the Nazi Party.
- To keep records of any suspected opponents.

The Gestapo

Full name: *Geheime Staatspolizei* or State Secret Police
Leader: Reinhard Heydrich
Number of employees: Around 30,000 by 1944
Their role:
- To spy on people to find out who opposed the Nazis.
- Used phone 'taps' to listen in on what individual people were saying, and searched homes.
- In 1939 alone, 160,000 people were arrested by the Gestapo.

Other information:
- Had no uniforms and worked in secret so nobody could be sure who they were.
- This made people very scared to say anything bad about the Nazis.
- Used torture to get people to confess to crimes.
- Could imprison people without trial and send them to concentration camps.

Source C

Instructions to the Gestapo from their deputy chief, Werner Best.

Any attempt to... uphold different ideas will be ruthlessly dealt with, as the symptoms of an illness which threatens the healthy unity of the state. To discover the enemies of the state, watch them and render them harmless is the duty of the political police.

Source A

Himmler addressing the Committee for Police Law in 1936.

It does not matter in the least if our actions are against some clause in the law; in my work for the Führer and the nation, I do what my conscience and common sense tells me is right.

Source B

Himmler, speaking to SS commanders, 18 February 1937.

In the SS we have about one case of homosexuality a month. They will be publicly degraded, expelled, and handed over to the courts... they will be sent to a concentration camp*, and shot, while attempting to escape. Thereby, the healthy blood which we are cultivating for Germany, will be kept pure.

Key terms

Pure German*

The Nazis believed that Germans should only marry and have children with other Germans. They did not believe that Jews and other minority groups were 'true' Germans (even though many had been born and raised in Germany, and spoke German).

Concentration camp*

A place where large numbers of people were imprisoned and usually forced to work. Conditions in concentration camps were often appalling and many prisoners in the camps died.

Some historians believe that the fear of Hitler's police forces was even more powerful than the police forces themselves. There were only 30,000 Gestapo to police a population of about 80 million. Because of this, they had to rely on informants and the support of ordinary citizens (see Interpretation 1).

Source D

A photograph of Nazi stormtroopers in the German city of Stuttgart. Their banner reads 'We won't tolerate* sabotage* of the work of the Führer'.

Interpretation 1

From *The Nazis: A Warning from History*, by Laurence Rees, published in 2005.

Like all modern policing systems, the Gestapo was only as good or bad as the co-operation it received – and the files reveal that it received a high level of co-operation. Only around 10% of political crimes committed… were actually discovered by the Gestapo; another 10% were passed on to the Gestapo by the regular police or the Nazi Party. Around 80% was discovered by ordinary citizens who turned the information over… Most of this unpaid cooperation came from people who were not members of the Nazi Party – they were 'ordinary' citizens.

Exam-style question, Section A

Explain why the Nazi police state was successful between 1933 and 1939.

You may use the following in your answer:

• the Gestapo

• concentration camps.

You must also use information of your own. **12 marks**

Exam tip

Focus on explaining 'why'. Aim to give at least three clear reasons. Two reasons have been given for you: the Gestapo and concentration camps. For each of these, try to write three or four sentences explaining how the Nazis used these things to create a police state.

Next, using your own knowledge, think of another reason why the Nazis were successful in creating a police state. Write three or four sentences about that third reason.

Key terms

Tolerate*

To put up with something.

Sabotage*

To damage or undermine something.

Concentration camps

By 1939, 150,000 people had been arrested in Germany for doing things that the Nazis disapproved of, such as criticising Hitler or the Nazi Party.

The people who were arrested were sent to a new type of prison called **concentration camps**. They were run by the SA and the SS.

Concentration camps

The first concentration camp was set up in 1933, at Dachau. A camp for women was set up at Moringen in 1933.

The concentration camps were far away from cities so that few people could see what was happening inside.

Those sent to the camps were:
- 'undesirables'* such as prostitutes and homosexuals
- minority groups that the Nazis disapproved of, such as the Jews
- political prisoners who the Nazis thought might oppose their control of Germany. They included communists and political writers (see Source E).

Figure: The Nazis set up a new type of prison.

Source E

A photograph of Carl von Ossietzky, a journalist and critic of the Nazis, at Esterwegen concentration camp in 1935.

Controlling the legal system

Another way that Hitler controlled his police state was by controlling what happened within the legal system*.

Controlling the judges

Firstly, Hitler set up the National Socialist League for the Maintenance of the Law. All judges were forced to be members. If any judges displeased the Nazis, they were denied membership. Judges were told that the interests of the Nazi Party were more important than the law (see Source F).

Source F

A speech by Hans Frank from 1936. Hitler appointed Frank as President of the German Academy of Law.

The basis for interpreting all legal sources is the Nazi philosophy, especially as expressed in the party programme and in the speeches of our Führer.

Controlling the law courts

Next, Hitler abolished trial by jury*. Judges decided who was innocent, who was guilty and what the punishment should be.

Finally, Hitler set up a new People's Court, to hear all cases of crimes against the state. Judges for this court were hand-picked and trials were held in secret. Hitler sometimes sentenced people himself (see Source G). Between 1934 and 1939, 534 people were sentenced to death for political offences.

Source G

A letter from Hitler's private office, sent to the Gestapo. Luftgas was 74 years old. He had been convicted of hoarding eggs soon after the start of the Second World War.

The Führer has seen the press cutting about the sentencing of the Jew, Markus Luftgas, to 2½ years in prison. He desires that Luftgas should be executed. Please make the arrangements.

Key terms

Legal system*

How people are treated when they commit a crime, including the way the courts operate.

Trial by jury*

This is where, in court, a group of ordinary people decide if someone is guilty or not of a crime (based upon the evidence presented in a trial). It is considered to be a very fair system.

Activity ?

Write a list of three ways in which Hitler used the legal system to control Nazi Germany.

Controlling religious views

The Christian religion was another part of German society which the Nazi police state set out to control. At first, Hitler tried to control the Christian churches by encouraging them to work with the Nazi government (see Sources H and I). When this did not work, he used the police state to attack Christians.

(see Sources H and I)

Source H

Extracts from a speech by Hitler in the Reichstag on the Enabling Law, March 1933.

Christianity is the unshakeable foundation of the moral and ethical life of our people. The National Government's concern will be for cooperation of the Church with the State. It expects, however that (this) will meet with similar appreciation from their side.

The Catholic Church

They should worship me, not the Pope.

- One third of Germans were Catholic.
- Their loyalty was to the Pope more than it was to Hitler.
- Catholic children went to Catholic schools that taught Christian beliefs, not Nazi ones.

I will not stop Catholics from worshipping, nor close their schools.

In return, I shall tell the Catholic priests in Germany not to interfere in politics and to swear loyalty to the Nazis.

In 1933, Hitler and the Pope came to an agreement called a 'concordat'.

But Hitler did not keep to the agreement.

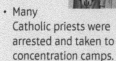

- Many Catholic priests were arrested and taken to concentration camps.
- Many Catholic schools were closed.
- Catholic youth groups were banned.

Figure: Hitler and the Catholic Church.

Source I

An NSDAP poster from 1933 showing the swastika knocking out the Catholics and the Communists.

Source J

Extract from the oath of allegiance (a promise of loyalty) to the Nazi regime, sworn by German Catholic bishops in 1933.

In my spiritual office, for the welfare and interest of the German Reich, I will endeavour to avoid all detrimental acts which might endanger it.

Source K

A French cartoon from 1933. The Pope is shown on the right, encouraging a priest to accept Hitler.

The Protestant Church

At first, some Protestants were so grateful that Hitler had protected them from anti-Christian Communists that they worked with the Nazis (see Source L).

The Reich Church, 1936

The Protestant churches which supported the Nazis came together in 1936 to form a single Protestant church called the Reich Church.

- Protestant pastors* who supported Hitler's views were allowed to continue giving church services.
- Some Protestant pastors even allowed the Nazi swastika to be displayed in their churches.

However, not all Protestants accepted the Nazi state. A few even spoke out against Hitler. The most famous of these was Pastor Martin Niemöller. In 1937, because of his opposition to the Nazis, Niemöller was sent to a concentration camp (see pages 100–101).

How far did Hitler succeed?

Hitler tried, at first, to work with the Christian churches. However, there was resistance in the churches to Nazi ideas. Just like the police and the law courts, they became 'Nazified'*.

Germany was becoming a **totalitarian state** – a country where the government controlled all sections of the state, including the Reichstag, the NSDAP, the army, the police and the legal system.

Source L

A statement from a German Protestant church leader in June 1937.

We all know that, if the Third Reich were to collapse, Communism would come in its place. So, we must show loyalty to the Führer, who has saved us from Communism and given us a better chance.

Key terms

Pastor*
A Protestant priest.

Nazified*
To become increasingly controlled by the Nazi Party.

Activities

1   Work with a partner to identify and write down:

　　a　two examples of Nazi Germany co-operating with the Christian churches

　　b　three examples of the Christian churches being oppressed in Nazi Germany.

2   Pages 83–89 are all about ways in which Hitler controlled Germany, using police, prisons, courts and religious changes. Draw a mind map containing all these key areas showing how they combined to create Hitler's police state. In order to do so, draw a spider diagram with a central heading 'Controlling Nazi Germany', with four branches and headings: police, prisons, courts, religion. Then, for each of the four headings, try to record three bullet points to summarise how the Nazis used each of these areas to control Germany.

Summary

- Nazi Germany was a police state, controlled by the SS, SD and Gestapo.
- From 1933, concentration camps were also used to deal with 'undesirables', such as political opponents of Nazism.
- The legal system was 'Nazified' – it was made to work in the interests of the Nazi Party. Law courts and judges were placed under the direct control of the Nazis.
- Religion was also closely controlled, although the Catholic and Protestant Churches did not agree with Nazi ideas.

Checkpoint

Strengthen

S1 Describe the key features of the SS, SD, Gestapo and concentration camps.

S2 How did the Nazi Party control Germany's legal system?

S3 How did the Nazi Party try to control religion in Germany?

Challenge

C1 Explain, using examples, why Nazi Germany is called a police state.

How confident do you feel about your answers to these questions? If you are unsure, look again at pages 83–86 for S1, page 87 for S2 and pages 88–89 for S3; for C1, join together with others and discuss a joint answer. Your teacher can provide hints.

3.3 Controlling and influencing attitudes

Learning outcomes

- Understand how Goebbels used propaganda to control and influence German people.
- Understand how the Nazis used media, sport, rallies, culture and the Arts to control and influence German people.

In Hitler's totalitarian state*, the Nazi Party tried to control the attitudes of the German people. It did this by:

- censorship*
- propaganda*
- controlling culture and the Arts.

Key terms

Totalitarian state*

A country where the ruling party controls everything, such as the police, the government, the army, the law, the religion and much else.

Censorship*

Censorship involves banning information or ideas. It sometimes involves banning newspapers, pictures, radio or film. Censorship therefore controls attitudes by stopping certain information or opinions.

Propaganda*

Propaganda is another way of controlling attitudes, but propaganda doesn't ban opinions, it *creates* them. Propaganda uses things like newspapers, posters, radio and film, to put ideas into people's minds and therefore change their attitudes.

Goebbels and propaganda

- In 1933, Hitler made Joseph Goebbels the Minister of Propaganda.
- He was in charge of using the media, sport, culture and the Arts to spread Nazi ideas.
- He ensured that ideas and attitudes that the Nazis did not like were censored.
- He carefully buried Nazi ideas in what people read and saw, so that they often didn't notice them (see Source C).
- He was very important in controlling attitudes in Nazi Germany.

Source A

Joseph Goebbels speaking at a Nazi rally in 1938.

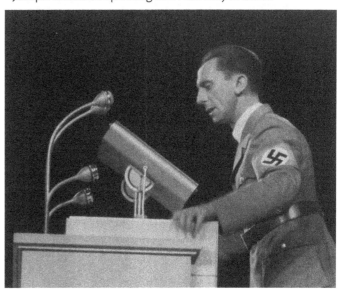

Source B

Hitler writing in *Mein Kampf* (Hitler's autobiography) in 1925.

The purpose of propaganda is to convince the masses. Their slowness of understanding needs time to absorb information. Only constant repetition will finally succeed in imprinting an idea on the mind.

Source C

Goebbels explaining the use of propaganda.

The finest kind of propaganda does not reveal itself. The best propaganda is that which works invisibly, penetrating every cell of life in such a way that the public has no idea of the aims of the propagandist [person creating the propaganda].

Activities ?

1 Write a sentence explaining why the Nazis used propaganda.

2 Using pages 92-98, write three or four sentences explaining the different types of propaganda the Nazis used. Write about at least three of the following: newspapers, radio, rallies, sport and/or art.

3 Which method of propaganda (newspapers, radio, rallies, sport or art) do you think would have had the biggest impact on the German people? Why?

Extend your knowledge

Joseph Goebbels

Joseph Goebbels was not a typical Nazi leader. He had not fought in the First World War, as many leading Nazis had. Goebbels was short and had a bad foot, which made walking difficult. He was an intelligent man and very well educated. He was angry about how Germany was treated in the Treaty of Versailles in 1919 (see page 17).

Goebbels joined the Nazi Party in 1922.

In 1930, Goebbels became the Nazi Party's Head of Propaganda. He organised the Nazi Party election campaigns.

When the Nazis came to power in Germany, Goebbels was Minister for People's Enlightenment and Propaganda. As well as being a superb organiser, he was a good speaker, presenting Nazi policy at rallies and on the radio.

Nazi use of the media

The press

Newspapers were common in Nazi Germany – but they had to put forward Nazi views, or they would be punished.

- Journalists were sometimes told what they could not say. This was censorship (see Source D).
- They were also given regular briefings, which were instructions telling them what they should write about. This was propaganda (see Source E).

Any newspapers that criticised Nazi views were closed down. In 1935, 1,600 newspapers were closed down. Every newspaper became a Nazi newspaper.

Source D

Ministry of Propaganda order, 1935.

Photos showing Reich government ministers at dining tables with rows of bottles must not be published in future.
This has given the absurd impression that members of the government are living it up.

Source E

General Instruction No. 674, given to the press in September 1939 by the Ministry of Public Enlightenment and Propaganda.

In the next issue, there must be a lead article, featured as prominently as possible, in which the decision of the Führer, no matter what it may be, will be discussed as the only possible one for Germany.

Radio

In the 1920s and early 1930s, Goebbels had started to use the power of the radio in Nazi election campaigns. Before televisions became available, everyone listened to the radio. After 1933, Goebbels censored radio stations and used them to broadcast* Nazi propaganda.

- All radio stations were put under Nazi control.
- Hitler and other Nazi officials made frequent broadcasts (see Source F).
- Cheap radios were sold to the public. They were also placed in cafés, factories and schools. Speakers were even placed in the street.

Source F

Ministry of Propaganda order, March 1934.

Attention! On Wednesday 21 March, the Führer is speaking on all German [radio] stations from 11 a.m. to 11.50 a.m... All factory owners, stores, offices, shops, pubs and flats must put up speakers an hour before, so that the whole workforce can hear.

Nazi use of rallies

Goebbels organised huge rallies* to show people the power and popularity of the Nazi Party, as well as the unity of Germany. For example, a huge rally was held each year at Nuremberg.

Exam-style question, Section A

Study Source F.

Give **two** things you can infer from Source F about Nazi propaganda. **4 marks**

Exam tip

This question tests source analysis, specifically the skill of making inferences.

A good answer will work out what can be inferred about Nazi propaganda using selected details in the source. Begin by saying what the source implies about Nazi propaganda, then add a quote to support your point. For example, 'Source F suggests Nazi propaganda was... It suggests this when it says...'

Repeat this process.

Key terms

Broadcast*

To transmit a radio programme.

Rally*

A large gathering of people who come together to show their support.

Thousands of swastika banners surrounded the rally ground

There were over 20,000 flags

130 anti-aircraft lights shone high into the air

200,000 people attended the rally

Hitler made speeches to the crowd

Figure: The Nuremberg rally of 1934.

Nazi use of sport

Goebbels also used sport to increase support for the Nazi Party and Nazi ideas (see Source G). He did this by 'Nazifying' sport. This meant:

- covering sports stadiums with Nazi symbols
- making all teams – including visiting teams from abroad – give the Nazi straight-armed salute during the German national anthem
- saying that sports victories were victories for Nazi values, such as aiming to be the best.

The Berlin Olympics of 1936

Hitler used sport as propaganda and to show Nazi Germany in a good light in 1936, when the Olympic Games were held in Germany.

The Nazis built an Olympic stadium in Berlin – the largest in the world.

All the events were very well organised, to show Nazi efficiency.

It was covered in swastikas and Nazi symbols.

Germany won 33 medals – more than any other country.

The games were filmed by one of Germany's leading film directors, Leni Riefenstahl. The films were used for Nazi propaganda.

Figure: The Olympic Games of 1936.

Source G

A statement by Joseph Goebbels in April 1933.

German sport has only one task: to strengthen the character of the German people, imbuing* it with the fighting spirit and comradeship* needed in the struggle for existence.

Key terms

Imbuing*

To inspire a feeling in someone.

Comradeship*

The company and friendship of others who share your beliefs.

Activities ?

1 Make a table with two columns, headed 'Censorship' and 'Propaganda'. In the columns, list all the ways the Nazis attempted to control – by censorship, or propaganda – the attitudes of the German people.

2 'Nazification of Germany' means that the Nazis tried to control all aspects of German life. Write a list of examples of Nazification including information on religion, sport and the legal system.

Source H

A photograph of German football fans giving the Nazi salute during an international match against England, December 1935.

Nazi control of culture and the Arts

The Nazis did not like much of the art that had been created during the period of the Weimar Republic (see pages 36–38). Instead, they liked art that showed:

- traditional ideas about Germany's past, such as country life and strong families
- Nazi values, like loyalty, struggle, self-sacrifice and discipline.

In 1933, the Nazis set up the Reich Chamber of Culture, led by Joseph Goebbels. The Chamber made sure that all art and culture supported the ideas of the Nazis.

- Art and activities that did not support Nazi ideas were banned.
- Over 12,000 works of art were removed from galleries.
- Artists had to get permission from the Chamber to sell their works or teach art.
- Competitions run by the Chamber rewarded artists who produced art that the Nazis liked (such as that in Source J).
- The Gestapo made surprise visits to artists' studios to check they were following the Chamber's rules.

Interpretation 1

From the website of the US Holocaust Memorial Museum, opened in 1993 to record details of the treatment of the Jews by Nazi Germany.

One of the first tasks Nazi leaders undertook when they came to power in early 1933 was the synchronization [bringing into line] of all professional and social organizations with Nazi ideology and policy. The arts and cultural organizations were not exempt [free from having to do something] from this effort. Joseph Goebbels, the Minister for Popular Enlightenment and Propaganda, immediately strove to bring the artistic and cultural communities in line with Nazi goals.

Source I

From an official Nazi government letter to a German artist. Six hundred and eight of his paintings were also confiscated.

```
I hereby expel you from the National Chamber
of Fine Arts and forbid you, effective
immediately, any activity, professional or
amateur, in the field of graphic arts.
```

Source J

A painting called *The Führer Speaks*, by Paul Padua, produced in 1939. It shows a family listening to a radio broadcast by Hitler.

95

Architecture in Nazi Germany

The Nazis also had strong ideas about architecture*. They wanted buildings that made Nazi Germany seem powerful.

Hitler's favourite architect was Albert Speer.

Speer used design features which shaped people's ideas of Germany and the Nazi Party.

- He built huge buildings, so that size gave a sense of power.
- He also used building ideas from Ancient Rome and Ancient Greece, so that the buildings seemed grand and historic.
- He decorated his buildings with massive Nazi flags. This was to show the importance of the Nazi Party in all things.

Music in Nazi Germany

The Nazis also tried to control music in Germany. Some types of music were censored. For example, jazz music was banned, as it was seen as the work of black people whom the Nazis thought were inferior people.

Other types of music were encouraged because they supported parts of German culture which the Nazis liked. For example:

- the music of Richard Wagner, a famous German composer, was liked by the Nazis because his music was about heroic and powerful Germans from the past
- traditional German folk music was also popular.

Key term
Architecture*
The design of buildings.

Source K

A photograph, taken in 1938, of a building designed by Albert Speer for the Nazi Party rallies at Nuremberg.

Literature in Nazi Germany

The Nazis also had strong ideas about literature*.

- No new books could be published without permission from the Chamber of Culture.
- Books containing views which the Nazis didn't like were censored. As many as 2,500 writers were banned.
- Millions of books were taken from universities and libraries and burned on huge, public bonfires (see Source L).

Source M

A photograph of Nazi supporters burning books in Berlin on 10 May 1933.

Source L

Extracts from the 'Twelve Theses against the Un-German Spirit', which set out guidelines to German university students on banned literature. These guidelines were posted around German universities in May 1933.

1. It is the German Volk's [people's] responsibility to assure that its language and literature are the pure expression of its traditions.

2. At present there is a chasm [gap] between literature and German tradition. This situation is a disgrace.

4. Our most dangerous enemy is the Jew and those who are his slaves.

5. A Jew can only think Jewish. If he writes in German, he is lying. The German who writes in German, but thinks un-German, is a traitor!

Key term

Literature*
Writing and books.

Film in Nazi Germany

Goebbels also had control over the German film industry and tried to make sure that films supported Nazi ideas.

- A short film, called a newsreel, produced by the Nazis would have to be shown before any other film shown in a cinema. These newsreels were propaganda to show the achievements of the Nazi Party.
- All film-makers had to send details of the story of every new film to Goebbels for approval.

- The Nazi Party also made its own films. In total, they made about 1,300 films. They had underlying messages that supported Nazi ideas.
- Nazi films were propaganda. A popular cartoon in Nazi Germany featured Hansi the canary. Hansi was the hero. He was drawn to look like Hitler. Hansi's enemies in the cartoon were black crows. The crows represented Jewish people.

Activities

1 Continue the table you started on page 94.
   a Under the heading 'Censorship', list all the ways in which the Nazis banned cultural activity they didn't like.
   b Under the heading 'Propaganda', list the ways they used culture to spread Nazi ideas and attitudes.
2 Look at Source J on page 95. Why do you think the Nazi Party would have approved of it? (Remember that the Nazis liked traditional family values.)

Summary

- In Nazi Germany, censorship and propaganda were used to control and influence attitudes.
- Joseph Goebbels, head of the Ministry of People's Enlightenment and Propaganda, was the co-ordinator of Nazi censorship and propaganda.
- The Nazis used the media, rallies and sport, including the Olympic Games, to control and influence attitudes.
- The Nazis also controlled the Arts, including art, architecture, literature and film.

Checkpoint

Strengthen

S1 Explain what the terms censorship and propaganda mean.
S2 How did the Nazis use newspapers and radio to influence attitudes?
S3 How did the Nazis use rallies for propaganda?
S4 How did the Nazis use sport to influence attitudes in Germany?
S5 Describe how the Nazis controlled the Arts, including art, architecture, literature and film.

Challenge

C1 Do you think that the Nazis influenced ideas in Germany the most through censorship, or through propaganda?

How confident do you feel about your answers to these questions? If you are unsure, look again at pages 91–92 for S1, page 93 for S2 and S3, page 94 for S4 and pages 95–97 for S5; for C1, join together with others and discuss a joint answer. Your teacher can provide hints.

3.4 Opposition, resistance and conformity

- Understand the different groups of people who resisted the Nazis, including resistance from the Church and young people.

Support for the Nazi regime

There was a lot of support amongst German people for Hitler and the Nazis. Amongst most Germans there was a high level of **conformity**, or acceptance, of Hitler and the Nazis and their policies.

- One reason was censorship and propaganda. Joseph Goebbels banned criticism of the Nazis and used the media to spread positive messages about them.

- Another reason was Nazi success. For example, during the 1930s, Hitler reduced unemployment.

However, there were several areas of opposition to the Nazis, shown in Figure 3.2.

Key term

Trade union*

An organised group of workers, who act together to protect their rights.

Secret trade union* opposition
Workers sometimes opposed Nazi building projects by staying off work sick or by damaging machinery.

Opposition amongst the young
Some young people (such as the Edelweiss Pirates) were opposed to Nazi youth groups.

Opposition to the Nazis

Secret political opposition
Some political opponents of the Nazis continued to operate in secret. The Social Democrats produced an anti-Nazi newspaper, but their leaders were arrested and sent to concentration camps.

Opposition amongst the Churches
Because the Nazis tried to control religion in Germany, many religious leaders opposed them.

Secret army opposition
Some army officers opposed the Nazis. One army general called Ludwig Beck tried to get fellow officers to arrest Hitler. He led plots to kill Hitler in 1943 and 1944.

Figure 3.2 Opposition to Hitler and the Nazis.

Key terms

Idolise*

To greatly admire or respect someone.

Despondency*

To lose hope.

Degradation*

To break down.

Pastor*

A priest/minister in the Protestant Church.

Resistance and opposition

There was some resistance and opposition to the Nazis.

- **Resistance** means refusing to support something or speaking against it.
- **Opposition** means actively working against something in order to remove it.

Opposition from churches

Hitler and the Nazis tried to control religion in Germany (see pages 88–89).

- Catholic bishops had to swear loyalty to the Nazi regime; Catholic schools and Catholic youth groups were closed.
- Protestant pastors* also had to show their loyalty by joining the German Christian Church (or Reich Church), which supported the Nazis.

The Pastors' Emergency League (PEL)

In 1933, a group of Protestant pastors, including Martin Niemöller, set up the Pastors' Emergency League (PEL). They opposed the Nazi treatment of Protestant Churches in Germany.

The Confessing Church

In 1934, the PEL set up the Confessing Church. This meant there were two Protestant Churches in Germany (the Reich Church and the Confessing Church).

- The Reich Church agreed to let the Nazis have a say in how to run their Church.
- The Confessing Church opposed the Nazis having a say in the running of their Church.

Some pastors spoke out against the Nazis. About 800 were arrested and sent to concentration camps.

Catholic opposition

Some Catholic priests also spoke out against Nazi ideas and policies. Around 400 Catholic priests were eventually imprisoned in Dachau concentration camp.

The limits of Church opposition

Although many Church leaders did voice opposition to the Nazis, their opposition was limited (see Interpretation 1). Opposition to the Nazis amongst ordinary Christians was also limited. There were few Christians who were brave enough, or foolish enough to oppose the Nazis openly.

Interpretation 1

From *The Nazi Dictatorship*, by Ian Kershaw, published in 1985.

The Churches offered less than fundamental resistance to Nazism. Their energies were used in opposing Nazi interference with their traditional practices. This was not matched by equally vigorous denunciation* of Nazi inhumanity* and barbarism*.

Key terms

Denunciation*

To openly oppose and criticise something.

Inhumanity*

Extremely cruel behaviour.

Barbarism*

Uncivilised behaviour - like a barbarian.

Source B

Part of a lesson used frequently by Martin Niemöller in sermons and speeches. He used it to condemn Church leaders who did little to speak out against the evils of Nazi Germany in the 1930s.

First they came for the Socialists, and I did not speak out — because I was not a Socialist.

Then they came for the Trade Unionists, and I did not speak out — because I was not a Trade Unionist.

Then they came for the Jews, and I did not speak out — because I was not a Jew.

Then they came for me — and there was no one left to speak for me.

Activities

1 Make a table with two columns. In one column, list ways in which Christian Churches in Germany resisted or opposed Hitler and the Nazis. In the other column, list ways in which they didn't.

2 Write three bullet points to show what Martin Neimoller's story shows us about opposition in Nazi Germany.

The role of Pastor Martin Niemöller

During the First World War, Martin Niemöller had been a German U-boat (submarine) commander. Later, he became a Protestant pastor.

"The Nazis have no right to try to run our Church."

He opposed the Nazis trying to run the Protestant Church in Germany. He was a founder of the PEL in 1933.

Figure: The part played by Pastor Niemöller in opposing the Nazis.

Niemöller discovered that, as a critic of the Nazis, his telephone had been bugged by the Gestapo. He was repeatedly arrested between 1934 and 1937.

In 1937, he was arrested by the Gestapo and charged with opposing the Nazi state. He was found guilty and imprisoned in a concentration camp. He remained a prisoner until 1945 when the Nazis were defeated in the Second World War.

Opposition from the young

In the 1920s, Hitler had made sections of the Nazi Party especially for young people, such as the Hitler Youth and the League of German Girls (see page 56). Eventually, all young people were expected to attend (see pages 115–118).

Most young Germans conformed*, but some young people were opposed to these Nazi youth groups.

Source C

A young man describing the activities and atmosphere at a Hitler Youth camp in 1938.

We hardly had any free time. Everything was done in a military way, from reveille [early morning bugle call], first parade, raising the flag, morning sport and ablutions [bathing], through breakfast to the 'scouting games', lunch and so on into the evening. Several participants left the camp because the whole slog was too stupid for them... Comradeship was very poor, and everything was done for command and obedience.

Source D

A photograph of Edelweiss Pirates from 1938.

Some young people wanted to have more freedom. They set up their own youth groups in opposition to the official Nazi groups. The best known were the Edelweiss Pirates and the Swing Youth.

The Edelweiss Pirates

The Edelweiss Pirates began in the late 1930s in working-class districts of big German cities.

- Groups took on fun names, such as the 'Travelling Dudes'.
- Their symbol was the white edelweiss flower.
- They were mostly teenage boys and girls.
- They did not like the rules and discipline of the Hitler Youth. They wanted fun and freedom.
- Boys wore their hair longer and copied American styles of clothing.
- To break away from Nazi rules, they went on long hikes in the countryside where they camped, sang songs and told jokes, sometimes mocking the Nazis.

Key term

Conform*

To go along with the rules and expected behaviours.

102

The Swing Youth

Another group that opposed the Nazis were the Swing Youth. The figure below shows some of their activities.

Members were teenagers from wealthy families. They came mainly from big cities like Berlin.

The Swing Youth was named after a type of music that was called 'swing'.

Members loved American music and culture:
- They danced the 'jitterbug', which came from America.
- They listened to jazz, which had been banned by the Nazis.

They held illegal parties, with drinking and smoking. There were 6,000 people at some of the parties.

Figure: The Swing Youth were popular with young people who opposed the Nazis.

Source E

From a report on the Swing Youth in 1939, carried out in 1944 by the Nazi Reich Ministry of Justice.

At the turn of 1939-40, the Flottbeck group (of Swing Youth) organised dances which were attended by 5,000 to 6,000 people and they were marked by an uninhibited indulgence* in swing... They regard Englishmen as the highest form of human development. A false conception of freedom leads them into opposition to the Hitler Youth.

Opposition or resistance?

Up to 1939, the opposition of the Edelweiss Pirates and the Swing Youth to the Nazis was limited.

- Their actions were limited. The Pirates and the Swing Youth were against Nazi ideas but, apart from sometimes telling anti-Nazi jokes and attacking members of the Hitler Youth, they did little to oppose the Nazis.
- Their aims were limited. They were more interested in music and fashion than politics.

- Their numbers were limited. By 1939, membership of the Edelweiss Pirates was about 2,000. The Hitler Youth had 8 million members.
- They were not typical of most of the German youth, who conformed to the Nazis' expectations.
- They were not a real threat to the Nazi Party.

Activities ?

1 List three reasons why some young Germans preferred to set up their own youth groups rather than attend Hitler Youth or the League of German Girls.

2 Work in pairs. One person should create a one-minute speech about the Edelweiss Pirates; the other a one-minute speech on the Swing Youth. After giving your speeches, both write three or four sentences recording the key points about each group.

Key term

Uninhibited indulgence*

Freely enjoying something – possibly too much.

Exam-style question, Section A

Explain why there was so little resistance and opposition to Hitler and the Nazis in Germany in the years 1933–39.

You may use the following in your answer:

- Nazi propaganda
- the Gestapo.

You **must** also use information of your own.   **12 marks**

Exam tip

A good answer will:

- include at least three factors which were reasons why there was so little resistance and opposition to Hitler and the Nazis
- have detailed information about how each reason restricted resistance and opposition.

Use the two factors that have been given – the Gestapo and Nazi propaganda. For each of these, try to write three or four sentences explaining how they stopped resistance to the Nazis.

Use your own knowledge to think of another factor that meant resistance to the Nazis was limited. Write four sentences about that third factor.

Summary

- Most Germans supported Hitler and the Nazis, or at least conformed to Nazi ideas.
- Opposition was limited because of Nazi propaganda and the Nazi police state, which stopped criticism of the Nazis.
- However, there was some resistance and opposition.
- Opposition came from some political groups, trade unions, the army, the Churches and youth groups.
- Some Church leaders opposed the Nazis, but they were in a minority and were punished.
- Some young people set up youth groups that they could join instead of the Nazi youth groups, but although they resisted Nazi ideas, their opposition was only small before 1939.
- Very few people were brave enough to oppose Hitler and the Nazis openly.

Checkpoint

Strengthen

S1 Explain what conformity, resistance and opposition are.

S2 Describe the opposition to the Nazis amongst political groups, trade unions and the army.

S3 What opposition was there to the Nazis by Church leaders?

S4 What opposition was there to the Nazis by German youth groups?

Challenge

C1 Explain why there was little opposition to the Nazis.

How confident do you feel about your answers to these questions? If you are unsure, look again at page 99 for S1–S2, pages 100–101 for S3 and pages 102–103 for S4; for C1, join together with others who want to consider the same question and discuss a joint answer. Your teacher can provide hints.

Recap: Nazi control and dictatorship, 1933–39

Recall quiz

1 When was the Reichstag Fire?
2 When was the Enabling Act?
3 When was the Night of the Long Knives?
4 Who was Hitler's head of the SS?
5 Name the Nazi leader who was put in charge of the SD and the Gestapo.
6 Who was Hitler's Minister of Propaganda?
7 What style of art did the Nazis approve of?
8 Who was the Protestant pastor who became a key critic of Nazi religious policies?
9 What was the name of the youth group which set up in opposition to the Hitler Youth and which used a white flower as its emblem?
10 What was the name given to the youth movement of young Germans who met to listen and dance to American music?

Activities ?

1 Write three or four sentences explaining why the Reichstag Fire was important.

2 List three ways in which the Enabling Act changed how laws were made in Germany. What was the effect of these changes?

3 On a sheet of A4 paper, draw a large set of weighing scales at the bottom of the page. Label the scales 'Controlling Nazi Germany'.

   a On one side of the weighing scales, list all the ways in which the Nazis controlled Nazi Germany by force – e.g. by police activity, by punishments or by banning things.

   b On the other side of the weighing scales, list all the ways in which the Nazis controlled Nazi Germany by persuasion – e.g. by propaganda or by agreements.

4 Identify two key differences between the Arts in the Weimar Republic and the Arts in Nazi Germany.

5 Look at the diagram on page 99 showing opposition to Hitler and the Nazis. Copy the diagram onto a sheet of A4 paper. Use the information on pages 100–103 to put brief details in the text boxes on 'Opposition amongst the Churches' and 'Opposition amongst the young'.

Exam-style question, Section A

Explain why Hitler was able to increase his control over Germany between 1933 and 1939.

You may use the following in your answer:

- the Enabling Act
- Nazi propaganda.

You **must** also use information of your own.   **12 marks**

Exam tip

A good answer will:

- include at least three factors which were reasons why Hitler was able to increase his control over Germany
- have detailed information about how each reason increased his control of Germany.

Use the two factors that have been given – the Enabling Act and Nazi propaganda. For each of these, try to write three or four sentences explaining how they allowed Hitler to increase his control.

Use your own knowledge to think of another factor that helped Hitler extend his control over Germany. Write four sentences about that third factor.

Writing historically: explaining and evaluating

Think about the purpose of your writing to help structure it and choose how you express your ideas.

Learning outcomes

By the end of this lesson, you will understand how to:

- use the key features of writing that explains or analyses something
- structure your writing to ensure you explain or evaluate effectively.

Definitions

Explain: to make an idea clear using relevant facts, details and examples.

Evaluate: to examine two or more points of view closely and carefully in order to make a judgement or come to a conclusion.

What are the similarities and differences in writing to **explain** and writing to **evaluate**?

Compare these two exam-style questions (note Question B has been adapted to make reference to Interpretation 2):

Question A

Explain why there was so little resistance and opposition to Hitler and the Nazis in Germany in the years 1933–39. **(12 marks)**

Question B

How far do you agree with Interpretation 1 (see page 136) about the events of *Kristallnacht* in 1938?

Explain your answer using Interpretations 1 and 2 (see page 136) and your knowledge of the historical context. **(16 marks)**

1. Look at the statements below. Which apply to Question A, which to Question B and which to both? This type of question:

   a. asks you to write to explain

   b. asks you to evaluate

   c. asks you to consider arguments for and against a point of view and reach a conclusion

   d. requires you to explain how and why an event happened or a situation came about

   e. requires you to provide evidence and examples to support your ideas

   f. requires you to link all your ideas to key points

   g. requires you to demonstrate good knowledge and understanding of the historical period.

2. Look at your answers to Question 1. What are the key differences between questions that ask you to 'explain' and questions that ask you 'how far do you agree'?

WRITING
HISTORICALLY

How can I structure writing to explain and writing to evaluate?

3. Answers to explain why questions often follow the structure: 1st point; 2nd point; 3rd point; summary.

The start of some sentences have been written out below in answer to Question A. Try to complete the sentences using your own knowledge.

> a. Once Hitler had the power to pass laws without the Reichstag, he set about removing other sources of opposition. He did this by...
>
> b. Goebbels' use of propaganda was important because...
>
> c. Hitler's control of culture and the Arts were another key reason for his success...

4. Now look at the plan below for an answer to an exam-style question that asks you to evaluate. Remember, in the exam you would need to refer to both interpretations in the question.

1st point to support the interpretation	a. In 1933, before Kristallnacht, the brownshirts (SA) had helped to enforce the official boycott of Jewish businesses, which...
2nd point to support the interpretation	b. These boycotts were still happening in 1938. Across Germany, the brownshirts would stand outside shops with banners discouraging people from entering...
Signal a turning point in the argument	c. However, Interpretation 1 does not take into account that many ordinary Germans did not actively take part in the destruction and violence...
1st point to contradict the interpretation	d. Many ordinary Germans were horrified by the destruction...
2nd point to contradict the interpretation	e. Opposition to Kristallnacht might not have been strong because people feared being arrested or killed...
Conclusion: a judgement directly responding to the interpretation	f. Interpretation 1 is correct in some things that it says, but I cannot agree with it fully because...

5. Look at these exam-style questions:

> Explain why Germany experienced recovery between 1924 and 1929. **(12 marks)**
>
> How far do you agree with Interpretation 3 about the reasons for the growth of support for the Nazi Party, 1929–1933?
>
> Explain your answer, using Interpretation 1 (on page 62) and Interpretation 3 (on page 64) and your knowledge of the historical context. **(16 marks)**

Plan an answer to each one, using the same structures as the responses above. Write the first sentence of each paragraph.

04 | Life in Nazi Germany, 1933–39

Many of the events described so far in this book have been **national** events, which happened to Germany – the German revolution, the Treaty of Versailles, the Weimar Republic and the start of the Nazi Third Reich.

Many of the people described so far in this book have been **national** figures, from the centre of political events – people like the Kaiser, Stresemann and Hitler.

The final section of this book is about the lives of **ordinary** Germans. For example, what was work and marriage like for German women in Nazi Germany? What was life like for children in Nazi Germany – and how did the Nazis view children? What was quality of life like for ordinary Germans?

Finally, this section will show what life was like in Nazi Germany for **minority** groups such as 'gypsies', Jews, Slavs, homosexuals and people with disabilities.

Learning outcomes

In this chapter you will learn about:

- Nazi views and policies towards women and the family
- Nazi aims and policies towards the young
- employment and the standard of living in Nazi Germany
- the persecution of minorities in Nazi Germany.

Chapter 1 showed what life was like for women in the Weimar Republic in the 1920s (see pages 34–35). This section is about what life was like for women under the Nazis in the 1930s.

Nazi views on women and the family

The Nazis believed that women should take on the traditional role of mother and housewife, while men provided money for the family. Figure 4.1 shows the three main views the Nazis had about women and the family.

Source A

Joseph Goebbels, a leading Nazi, describing the role of women in 1929.

The mission of women is to be beautiful and to bring children into the world. The female bird... hatches eggs for him. In exchange, the male takes care of gathering the food and stands guard and wards off [protects from] the enemy.

Source B

Hitler, addressing a Nazi rally in Nuremberg in 1934.

... one might say that the world of a woman is a smaller world. For her world is her husband, her family, her children and her house. But where would the greater world be with no one to care for the small world? Every child that a woman brings into the world is a battle waged for the existence of her people.

Source C

A painting from 1939 by Adolf Wissel, an official Nazi artist, showing a German family.

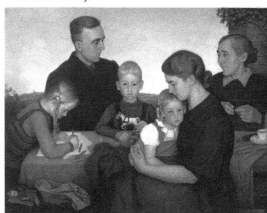

Appearance: Women should look 'natural' with simple plaited or tied-back hair and long skirts.

Employment: The Nazis wanted women to stay at home rather than go to work, so they could raise a family. They believed that men should earn the money for the family.

Marriage and family: The Nazis wanted women to marry and have as many children as possible, as more children would make Germany stronger. They believed that women should spend their lives looking after their family. They should learn household skills, like cooking.

Figure 4.1 Nazi views on women and the family.

Nazi policies towards women

The Nazi Party tried to influence the lives of ordinary Germans in order to create a society which reflected their beliefs. This included many policies aimed at shaping the role of women in German society.

Source D

A speech by Gertrud Scholtz-Klink, Reich Women's Leader, in 1936.

Not only will women with children become mothers of the nation - but every German woman and girl will become one of the Führer's little helpers, wherever she is.

Source E

Wilhelmine Haferkamp, a mother from the industrial city of Oberhausen, interviewed in the 1980s. She is describing the benefits she received for having many children – she eventually gave birth to 10.

I got 30 marks per child from the Hitler government and 20 marks from the city. That was a lot of money. I sometimes got more 'child money' than my husband earned... I was proud. When I got the gold [Mother's Cross medal], there was a big celebration in a school, where the mothers were all invited for coffee and cake.

Women's organisations

- Gertrud Scholtz-Klink (see Source D) was appointed Reich Women's Leader.
- She was in charge of the German Women's Enterprise (DFW).
- All women's groups had to be a part of the DFW.
- This meant that they had to follow Nazi beliefs.
- Any that did not, were closed down.

Gertrud Scholtz-Klink

Marriage and divorce

- The Law for the Encouragement of Marriage was introduced in 1933.
- This gave large loans to couples who married and had children.
- Money was only given if the wife stopped work.
- Divorce laws also changed. If a wife could not give birth to children, the husband could divorce her.

Nazi policies towards women

Childbirth

- Medals, called the 'Mother's Cross', were awarded to women who had many children.
- Couples having four children or more didn't need to pay back the marriage loan.
- A programme called *Lebensborn* ('Fountain of Life') was introduced. It encouraged single women to 'breed' with SS men.

Figure: Nazi policies towards women.

Extend your knowledge

Changing people's behaviour

Governments that want to change people's behaviour can't always do it by force. For example, the Nazis could not force women to have more children – but they could influence people's behaviour by changing the law.

For example, as well as receiving marriage loans, women could also get monthly payments from the government to help with the cost of bringing up children.

Activities ?

1. List three Nazi beliefs about marriage and the family.

2. For each Nazi belief on your list, note down policies on pages 110–111 which show what the Nazis did to try to change society to fit those beliefs. For example, they believed that women should be mothers (their belief), so they gave medals to women for having lots of children (what they did).

Women and employment

The Nazis wanted to reduce the number of women in work. They believed a woman should be in the home bringing up her family.

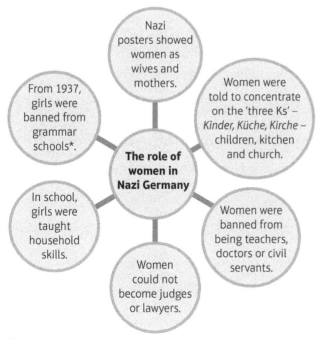

Figure: The role of women in Nazi Germany.

Source F

From an interview with Gertrud Draber in 2001, in which she is remembering what it was like to be a young woman in Nazi Germany.

Young girls from the age of ten onward were taught... to take care of their bodies, so they could bear as many children as the state needed... Birth control information is frowned on and practically forbidden.

My main aim as a woman was above all to become a mother. I wanted to be a perfect housewife. I wanted to do something different with my life, not just be a working girl in an office.

Source G

A photograph of girls in the League of German Girls from the 1930s, practising their domestic skills* in preparation for motherhood.

Key terms

Grammar schools*

Schools which prepared students for university.

Domestic skills*

Household skills, like cooking, sewing and cleaning.

The appearance of women in Nazi Germany

The Nazis never forced women to look a certain way through laws. However, Nazi propaganda did encourage women to look a certain way (see Source C on page 109). Women were encouraged to wear modest clothes, with their hair tied back, in plaits or in a bun. They were discouraged from dyeing their hair or wearing make-up.

How effective were Nazi policies towards women?

Nazi policies towards women had only mixed success. The table below shows the successes and the failures.

Successes of Nazi policies	Failures of Nazi policies
• Many women conformed (did as expected of them) • Fewer women went to university • Birth rates increased • Male employment increased, as women left the workforce	• Some women disliked Nazi ideas about womanhood (see Sources H, I and J) • By the end of the 1930s, the Nazis needed women to return to work as there was a shortage of workers

Source H

Traudl Junge was a young woman in Nazi Germany. Here she is remembering her youth in Nazi Germany.

Gertrud Scholtz-Klink was the type (of woman) we did not like at all. She was so ugly and wasn't fashionable. We didn't bother about joining her organisation. It didn't attract me or my friends. We were interested in dancing and ballet and didn't care much for political ideas.

Source I

Extract from a letter to a Leipzig newspaper in 1934.

A son, even the youngest, laughs in his mother's face. He regards her as his servant and women in general are merely willing tools of his aims.

Source J

A poster showing women as servants of the Nazi state. It was circulated by the Social Democratic Party – until the party was banned in 1933.

Activity

How effective do you think Nazi policies towards women were? Give them a mark out of 10. Discuss your mark – and your reasons – with other people in the class. Then write a short paragraph to explain the reasons for your mark.

Exam-style question, Section B

Study Sources F and J on pages 111–112.

How useful are Sources F and J for an enquiry into the attitudes of Germans towards Nazi policies towards women?

Explain your answer, using Sources F and J and your knowledge of the historical context.   **8 marks**

Exam tip

A good answer will consider:

- how useful the information in each source is for this particular enquiry. Consider what each of the two sources shows us about how Germans felt about Nazi policies towards women.

- how the provenance (i.e. the type of source, its origin, author or purpose) of each source affects how useful it is. For example, why might the authors of Source J be trying to show a negative view of Nazi policies towards women?

- how knowledge of Germany at this time affects a judgement of how useful each source is.

Summary

- The Nazis believed that women should have a traditional appearance, leave professional jobs to men and make marriage and motherhood their role.

- The Nazis used propaganda and policies to try to change society.

- The Nazis had several policies to encourage marriage and childbirth. These included the Law for the Encouragement of Marriage, changes to divorce law, the Mother's Cross and Lebensborn.

- The Nazis had several policies to reduce numbers of women in the workforce. These included banning women from some jobs and discouraging women from going to university.

- Some Germans believed in the Nazi policies towards women, but the policies had limited impact.

Checkpoint

Strengthen

S1 Describe Nazi ideas on marriage, motherhood and childbirth.

S2 Describe Nazi ideas about women and work.

S3 Describe Nazi policies on marriage, motherhood and childbirth.

S4 Describe Nazi policies on women and work.

Challenge

C1 Evaluate how effective you think Nazi policies towards women were.

How confident do you feel about your answers to these questions? If you are unsure, look again at page 109 for S1–S2, pages 110–111 for S3–S4; for C1, look again at page 112. If you are still unsure about a question, you could join together with others and discuss a joint answer. Your teacher can give you hints.

The aims of Nazi policies concerning the young

Nazi policies for the young had the aim of creating young people who worked hard for the benefit of the country.

Nazi policies towards the young were not meant to be what was best for young people. They were meant to strengthen Germany and strengthen the Nazi Party then and in the future.

There are two further things to note about the aims of Nazi policies towards the young.

1   The Nazis believed that boys and girls were equal, but different. Policies for boys were different from the policies for girls.

2   Nazi propaganda often encouraged young people to see Hitler as a father-figure. Source A shows an example of this.

Source A

This was one of a series of photograph cards for young Germans to collect, published in 1935. These cards could be pasted into a Nazi Party album, called *Adolf Hitler – Pictures of the Life of the Führer*.

All young Germans should be brought up to be proud Germans.

All young Germans should be brought up to be supporters of the Nazi Party.

What the Nazis believed was best for Germany

All girls should be brought up to be good future wives and healthy mothers.

All boys should be brought up to be strong and healthy. Later they should become good workers and strong soldiers for Germany.

Figure 4.2 The aims of Nazi policies towards the young.

The Nazi youth movement

Before Hitler became Chancellor in January 1933, there were many German youth groups for both boys and girls.

In 1933, however, Hitler banned almost all youth groups apart from Nazi groups.

In March 1939, all young Germans had to join Nazi youth groups from the age of 10. Only 'unwanted' minority groups, like Jews, were not made to join.

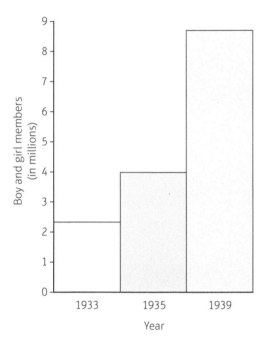

Figure 4.3 Number of 10 to 18 year-olds in Nazi Party youth groups, 1933–39.

Nazi youth groups for boys

Nazi youth groups were strictly segregated*, with separate groups for boys and girls. The group for 14 to 18 year-old boys was called the *Hitler Jugend* (Hitler Youth).

The Hitler Youth

Political training
Mainly, the Hitler Youth was a political group.

- Members had to swear an oath of loyalty* to the Führer.
- They had to attend courses and lessons where they were told about Nazi ideas, like the dangers posed by Jews.
- Hitler Youth members had to report anyone, even teachers and parents, who was disloyal* to the Nazis.

Hitler hoped to create a constant supply of Germans who were Nazi Party supporters.

Physical training
The Hitler Youth was also used by the Nazis to make young Germans as fit and healthy as possible.

- They regularly went camping and hiking.
- The Hitler Youth also ran sports competitions.

Key terms

Segregate*
To separate groups of people.

Oath of loyalty*
A promise to support someone.

Disloyal*
Someone who does not support something that they are expected to.

Military training

The Hitler Youth was organised to train young German boys to become good workers and strong soldiers. Military training was essential.

- Members practised skills useful to troops, such as map-reading and communications.
- By 1938, 1.2 million boys in the Hitler Youth were being trained in how to shoot guns.
- There were separate military divisions of the Hitler Youth for specialist training, including naval and flying training.

Source B

A photograph of rifle shooting practice for the Hitler Youth, taken in the 1930s.

Source C

An extract from a speech by Adolf Hitler in 1933.

My programme for youth is hard. Weakness must be hammered away... I want a brutal, domineering*, fearless, cruel youth. It must bear pain. There must be nothing weak and gentle about it... That is how I will create the New Order*.

Key terms

Domineering*

To dominate over other people.

New Order*

A vision for the future of a country.

Character training

The Hitler Youth was also designed to shape young people's characters.

- Its activities focused on the need for loyalty, competition and strength (see Source C).
- Training could be harsh: children might be plunged into ice-cold water or sent on long hikes in bad weather to toughen them up.
- There were harsh punishments for disobeying orders.

This was to build young Germans who would obey orders at all times.

The League of German Maidens

The Nazi Party created separate youth groups for girls. The group for 14 to 21 year-olds was called the *Bund Deutscher Maädal* (BDM), meaning the League of German Maidens.

The table shows the similarities and differences between the League of German Maidens and the Hitler Youth.

Similarities between the BDM and the Hitler Youth	Differences between the BDM and the Hitler Youth
• There were political activities, including rallies and oaths of loyalty (see Source D). • There were physical activities. For example, camping and marching were compulsory (see Source E).	• Girls did not do any military training. • Girls were trained to cook, iron and sew, to prepare them to be housewives. • Girls were also taught the importance of 'racial hygiene' – the idea that they should keep the German race 'pure' by only marrying Aryan* men.

Source D

A photograph of a BDM gathering in 1933. New members, with raised hands, swear allegiance to Hitler in front of the Nazi Youth Leader von Schirach.

Source E

A German woman, Ilse Mckee, remembering her time in the BDM. This was originally published in 1966, in a book of contemporary accounts (written at the time) of life in Nazi Germany between 1933 and 1939.

We had to be present at every public meeting and at youth rallies* and sports. The weekends were crammed full with outings, camping, and marches when we carried heavy packs on our backs. It was all fun in a way, and we certainly got plenty of exercise, but it had a bad effect on our school reports. There was hardly ever any time for homework.

... girls of my age had to attend evening classes twice weekly. The evening classes were conducted by young girls, usually hardly older than we were ourselves... we were of course lectured on a lot of Nazi ideology*, and most of this went over our heads... we were told from a very early age to prepare for motherhood, as the mother in the eyes of our beloved leader... was the most important person in the nation. We were Germany's hope and Germany's future.

Key terms

Aryan*

The Germanic race of people. The Nazis believed that Aryans were superior to all other races.

Rallies*

Large meetings and events where people gather to show their support for something.

Ideology*

A set of beliefs and ideas.

Did Nazi youth groups achieve Nazi aims?

Some young people were enthusiastic and loyal Hitler Youth members. However, some were less keen.

- Some children did not enjoy the activities they were forced to do.
- Many parents felt the Nazi youth groups taught loyalty to the Nazis, and not to the young person's family.

Sources F and G give differing views on the Hitler Youth.

Source F

A. Klonne, describing his memories of the Hitler Youth in his book, *Youth in the Third Reich*, published in 1982.

What I liked about the Hitler Youth was the comradeship*. I was full of enthusiasm. What boy isn't fired by ideals such as comradeship, loyalty and honour and the trips off into the countryside and sport? Later... negative aspects became obvious. The compulsion* and obedience were unpleasant. I preferred people to have a will of their own... In our troop, the activity was almost entirely boring military drill.

Source G

Henrik Metelmann was a member of the Hitler Youth in the 1930s. He wrote a book in 1980 explaining his experiences in Nazi Germany.

You felt you belonged to a great nation again. I was helping to build a strong Germany. But my father felt differently. He warned, "Henrik, don't tell them what I am saying to you." I argued with my father, because I was a great believer in the Hitler regime, which was against his background as a working man.

Key terms

Comradeship*

The company and friendship of others who are working together for a shared goal.

Compulsion*

Being forced to do something.

Activities ?

1 List the Nazis' aims for German youth.
2 Write two or three sentences to explain how the Nazis used youth groups for each of the following: a) political indoctrination*, b) military training, c) character building.

Interpretation 1

An extract from *Modern Germany*, by V. R. Berghahn (1982).

(The Hitler Youth's)... romantic appeal to a spirit of friendship and community, to sacrifice and the ideal of a well-ordered society, together with charismatic* leadership, met strong emotional needs among young people. There was also an element of rebellion against parents and teachers. So they went off, in Boy Scout fashion, to weekend camps and hikes, listening to the persuasive speeches of their leaders. It is not surprising that so many teenagers fell under the spell of the slogans by the fireside.

Exam-style question, Section B

Study Source F.

Give **two** things you can infer from Source F about the Hitler Youth.   **4 marks**

Exam tip

This question tests source analysis, specifically the skill of making inferences.

A good answer will work out what can be inferred (worked out) about the Hitler Youth using selected details in the source. For example you might write, 'Source F implies that the Hitler Youth was... It does so when it says that...', then take a quote from the source. Repeat this process twice.

Key terms

Indoctrination*

Brainwashing with ideas.

Charismatic*

A personal quality that makes other people like you.

Nazi control of the young through education

In 1933, all children in Germany went to school until the age of 14. Boys and girls went to separate schools.

Hitler wanted to control the schools in Germany because he believed that even if some adults did not believe in Nazi ideas, if children were taught from a young age to believe, they would follow Hitler, no matter what.

During the 1930s, the Nazis made a series of changes to bring all schools under their control.

Source H

An extract from Hitler's speech on May Day 1933.

When an opponent declares "I will not support you," I calmly say, "Your child belongs to us already. How important are you? You will soon be gone. Your children however now stand in our camp."

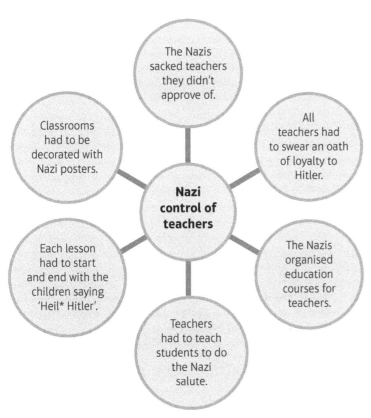

The Nazis sacked teachers they didn't approve of.

All teachers had to swear an oath of loyalty to Hitler.

Classrooms had to be decorated with Nazi posters.

Nazi control of teachers

The Nazis organised education courses for teachers.

Each lesson had to start and end with the children saying 'Heil* Hitler'.

Teachers had to teach students to do the Nazi salute.

Figure: Nazis controlled the education of young Germans by controlling the teachers.

Key term

Heil*

A German greeting and term of great respect.

Nazi control of the curriculum

The curriculum is what is taught in schools. Another way the Nazis controlled young Germans was to take control of the curriculum.

	Registration	Lesson 1	Lesson 2	Lesson 3	Lesson 4	Lesson 5	Lesson 6
Boys	Salutes and speeches	German	History	Race Studies	Physics and chemistry	PE: boxing, football and military drill	Maths
Girls	Salutes and speeches	German	History	Race Studies	Cooking and needlework	PE: dance and fitness	Maths

Every day began with salutes to Hitler. Children would be made to listen to Hitler's speeches on the radio.

The Nazis rewrote history textbooks, for example, telling students that it was Jews and Communists that had caused Germany to lose the First World War.

In this subject, children were told that Aryans were superior and that they should not marry other races, such as Jews, as they were said to be inferior.

The curriculum was different for boys and girls.

The amount of time in schools for PE was doubled. This was to make strong workers and soldiers, and healthy mothers.

Traditional subjects, like mathematics, were changed so that they spread Nazi ideas (see Source J).

Source J

A mathematics question from a German textbook approved by the Nazis.

A plane takes off carrying 12 bombs, each weighing 10 kilos. It bombs Warsaw, the world centre of Jews. At take-off, it had 1,500 kilos of fuel and weighed 8 tonnes. When it returned from its crusade, it had 230 kilos of fuel left. What was the weight of the aircraft?

Source I

A photograph taken in 1934 showing German students giving the Nazi salute.

THINKING HISTORICALLY Evidence (4a&b)

The 'weight' of evidence

One useful idea to have in mind when looking at historical sources is 'consistency' (whether or not sources support each other).

If a number of sources appear to suggest the same conclusion about the past, then we might feel more confident about accepting this conclusion.

However, we should not assume that just because an idea is in many sources, it must be correct. We should also consider the *nature* of the sources and the *reasons why* sources might seem to disagree.

Sources K and L could be used by a historian to build up a picture of how much political interference there was in schools under the Nazis.

1 Source K gives the impression that the Nazis controlled education very strictly. Does Source L give a similar, or different impression of education under the Nazis?

2 Why do you think that they say different things? Write down as many reasons as you can.

Discuss the following in groups:

3 If a historian had ten more sources that gave a similar impression to Source K and only four that agreed with Source L, would this mean that Source K was more truthful? Explain your answer.

4 What else should we consider, apart from 'the balance of the evidence' (the number of sources on each side), when making conclusions from sources such as these?

Source K

Extracts from *The Law for the Restoration of the Professional Civil Service*, 7 April 1933

The Reich Government has enacted [put in place] the following Law: ... civil servants [including teachers] may be dismissed from office in accordance with the following regulations.

Civil servants [including teachers] who have entered the service since November 9, 1918, without possessing the required or customary educational background or other qualifications are to be dismissed from the service.

Civil servants [including teachers] who are not of Aryan descent are to be retired.

Civil servants [including teachers] whose previous political activities suggest that they will not, at all times, give their fullest support to the national State, can be dismissed from the service.

Reich Chancellor Adolf Hitler

Source L

A school pupil comments on life in the mid 1930s.

No one in our class ever read *Mein Kampf*. I myself had only used the book for quotations.

In general we didn't know much about National Socialist ideas. Even anti-Semitism* was taught rather a little at school, for instance through Richard Wagner's essay 'The Jews in Music'. Outside school the display copies of *Der Stürmer* [a Nazi newspaper] made the idea seem ridiculous, if anything.

Nevertheless, we were politically programmed: programmed to obey orders, to cultivate the soldierly 'virtue' of standing to attention and saying 'Yes, Sir', and to switch our minds off when the magic word 'fatherland' was uttered and Germany's honour and greatness were invoked [brought up].

Key term

Anti-Semitism*

Hatred of Jews.

Activity ?

Make a table with the following headings.

Teaching Nazi beliefs	Making Germany stronger	Treating boys and girls differently

a   Using the information on pages 120–121, write as much as you can under each heading, giving examples of how the Nazis tried to achieve these aims in their schools.

b   When you have finished, write two or three sentences to explain what you think the main aims of schools in Nazi Germany were.

c   How does your conclusion fit with the ideas of Adolf Hitler?

Summary

- The Nazis believed that young Germans should be brought up to be useful Germans and supporters of Nazi ideas.
- They believed that boys and girls should be brought up to be different.
- Nazi youth groups, such as the Hitler Youth and the League of German Maidens, were organised to create strong, healthy Germans and supporters of Nazi ideas.
- Schools in Nazi Germany were organised to create useful German adults and Nazi supporters.
- The Nazis shaped the development of young Germans by controlling teachers and the curriculum.

Checkpoint

Strengthen

S1 Describe Nazi aims towards the young.

S2 How were Nazi youth groups organised?

S3 How were Nazi schools organised?

Challenge

C1 Explain how the features of Nazi youth groups were intended to achieve Nazi aims towards the young.

How confident do you feel about your answers to these questions? If you are unsure, look again at page 114 for S1, pages 115–118 for S2, pages 119–120 for S3. If you are still unsure about a question, you could join together with others and discuss a joint answer. Your teacher can give you hints.

4.3 Employment and living standards

Nazi policies to reduce unemployment

In January 1933, when Hitler became Chancellor, about five million Germans were unemployed. So reducing unemployment was a priority for Hitler. There were two reasons for this.

1   Unemployed workers suffered poor living conditions and demanded help. If Hitler could not help them, they might support the Communist Party instead.

2   The Nazis believed that unemployed workers were a waste of resources. They wanted as many people as possible in useful work, in the service of the country.

By 1939, unemployment had fallen to about half a million people (see Figure 4.4). How did the Nazis achieve this?

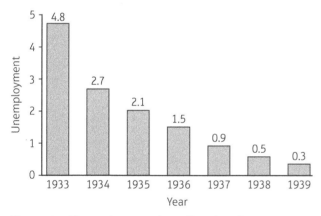

Figure 4.4 Unemployment (in millions) in Germany, 1933–39.

Labour Service (RAD)

In 1933, the Nazis set up the *Reichs Arbeits Dienst*, or RAD – the National Labour Service. This provided paid work for the unemployed. The table shows the benefits of the RAD and its limitations.

Benefits of the RAD	Limitations of the RAD
• It provided jobs, such as repairing roads and planting trees. • These projects were also good for Germany as a whole. • From 1935, all young men had to work for the RAD for six months. • In 1935 there were 422,000 in the RAD.	• It was not popular. • It was organised like an army – workers wore uniforms and lived in camps. • Pay was very low. • Working and living conditions were poor. • Some men saw the RAD as service for the Nazi Party, not real employment.

Source A

A photograph of Hitler greeting men in the Labour Service (RAD) at a Nazi Party rally in Nuremberg in 1938.

Autobahns and rearmament

The Nazis reduced unemployment through the building of motorways (the *autobahn*) and by increasing the size of Germany's armed forces (rearmament).

Construction: autobahns (motorways)

- The Nazis planned to build 7,000 miles of autobahns.
- Hitler personally started construction of the first autobahn (see Source B).
- 125,000 men were employed building autobahns.
- Better roads meant quicker transport for German industry and agriculture.
- This helped to boost the German economy.

Providing jobs

Rearmament: boosting Germany's military

- Hitler ignored the Treaty of Versailles, which had limited the size of Germany's armed forces, and aimed to expand them.
- From 1935, all young German men had to serve a period in the armed forces.
- By 1939, there were 1,360,000 men in the armed forces (see Figure 4.5).
- This helped to reduce the number of unemployed.
- Expanding the armed forces also created new jobs making weapons and uniforms.

Figure: Nazi policies to reduce unemployment.

Source B

A photograph taken in 1933. It shows Hitler personally 'turning the first turf' to start construction of the first autobahn.

Source C

From a speech by Hitler to his ministers in February 1933.

The next five years in Germany must be devoted to the rearmament of Germany. Every job creation scheme must be judged by whether it helps rearmament... Germany's position in the world will depend on the position of Germany's armed forces. Upon this, the position of Germany's economy also depends.

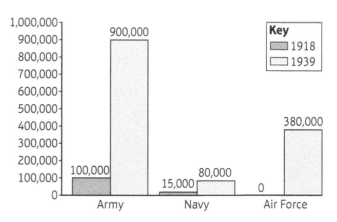

Key
- 1918
- 1939

Army: 100,000 / 900,000
Navy: 15,000 / 80,000
Air Force: 0 / 380,000

Figure 4.5 Size of the German armed forces, 1918–39.

Invisible unemployment

Some historians say that the Nazis didn't really reduce unemployment. They just found ways to reduce the number of people **recorded** as unemployed.

Figure 4.6 gives details of the ways that the Nazis 'hid' the real number of unemployed.

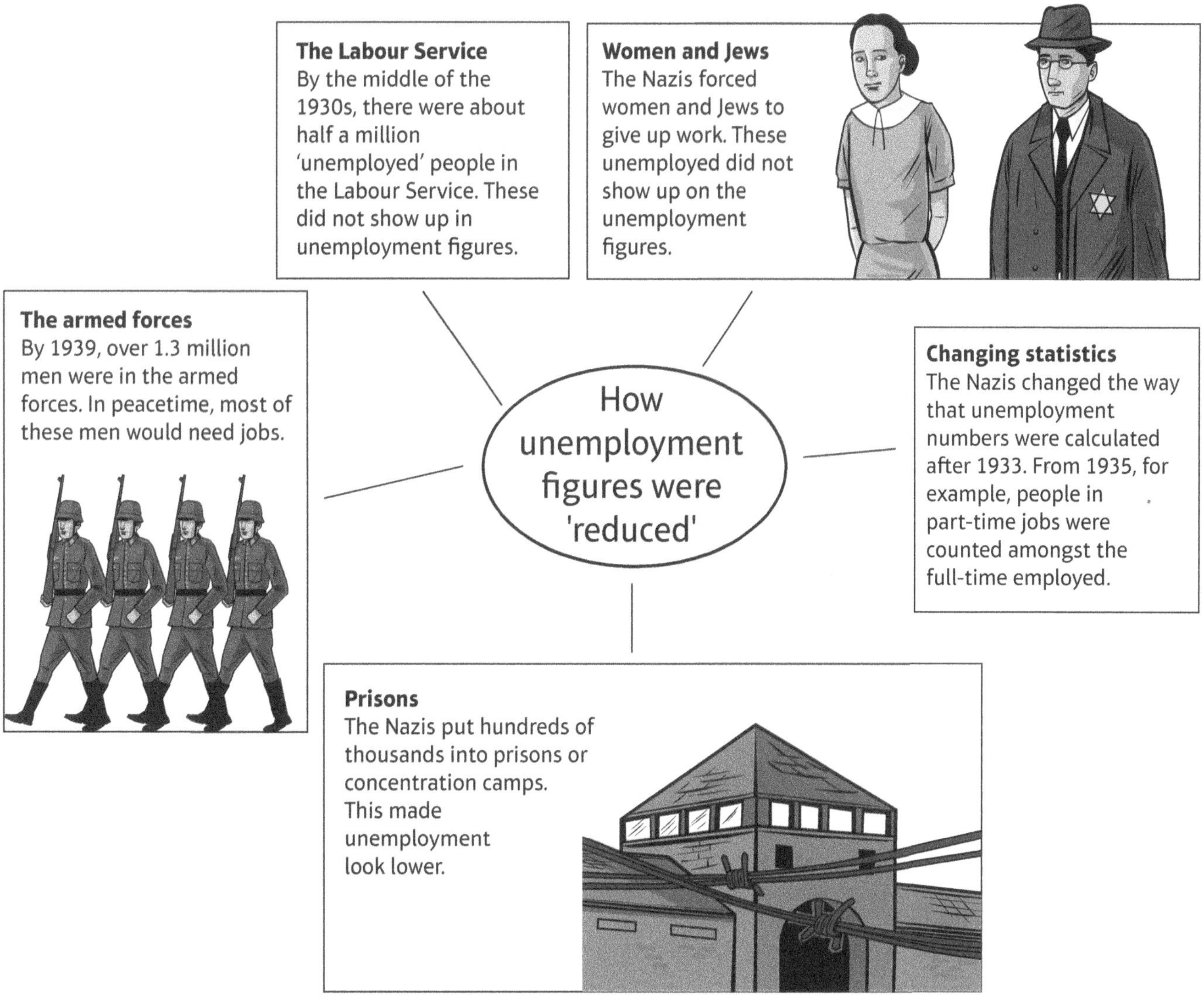

The Labour Service
By the middle of the 1930s, there were about half a million 'unemployed' people in the Labour Service. These did not show up in unemployment figures.

Women and Jews
The Nazis forced women and Jews to give up work. These unemployed did not show up on the unemployment figures.

The armed forces
By 1939, over 1.3 million men were in the armed forces. In peacetime, most of these men would need jobs.

How unemployment figures were 'reduced'

Changing statistics
The Nazis changed the way that unemployment numbers were calculated after 1933. From 1935, for example, people in part-time jobs were counted amongst the full-time employed.

Prisons
The Nazis put hundreds of thousands into prisons or concentration camps. This made unemployment look lower.

Figure 4.6 Ways in which the Nazis 'hid' the real level of unemployment.

Overall verdict on unemployment in Nazi Germany

The achievement of the Nazis in reducing the official unemployment figures in Germany by over four million was remarkable. However, it must be remembered that:

- unemployment was falling everywhere in the 1930s as countries recovered from the Great Depression
- some unemployed people, such as Jews, women and political prisoners, were not counted in official figures
- some jobs in Nazi Germany, such as building the motorways, cost the government a lot of money. The government would not have been able to afford this cost for long.

Activities	?

1   Give two reasons why Hitler wanted to reduce unemployment in Nazi Germany.
2   Write a list of the types of Germans who would have benefited from Nazi policies towards unemployment, and a list of the types of Germans who might have suffered.

Changes in the standard of living

The standard of living is a measure which tells us whether people's lives are getting better or worse. It is not easy to measure the changes in standard of living because:

- sometimes, the standard of living goes up for some people, but down for others
- sometimes, some aspects of people's lives get better and other aspects get worse
- sometimes people can become wealthier but their enjoyment of life gets worse.

With this in mind, what happened to the standard of living of German people in Nazi Germany?

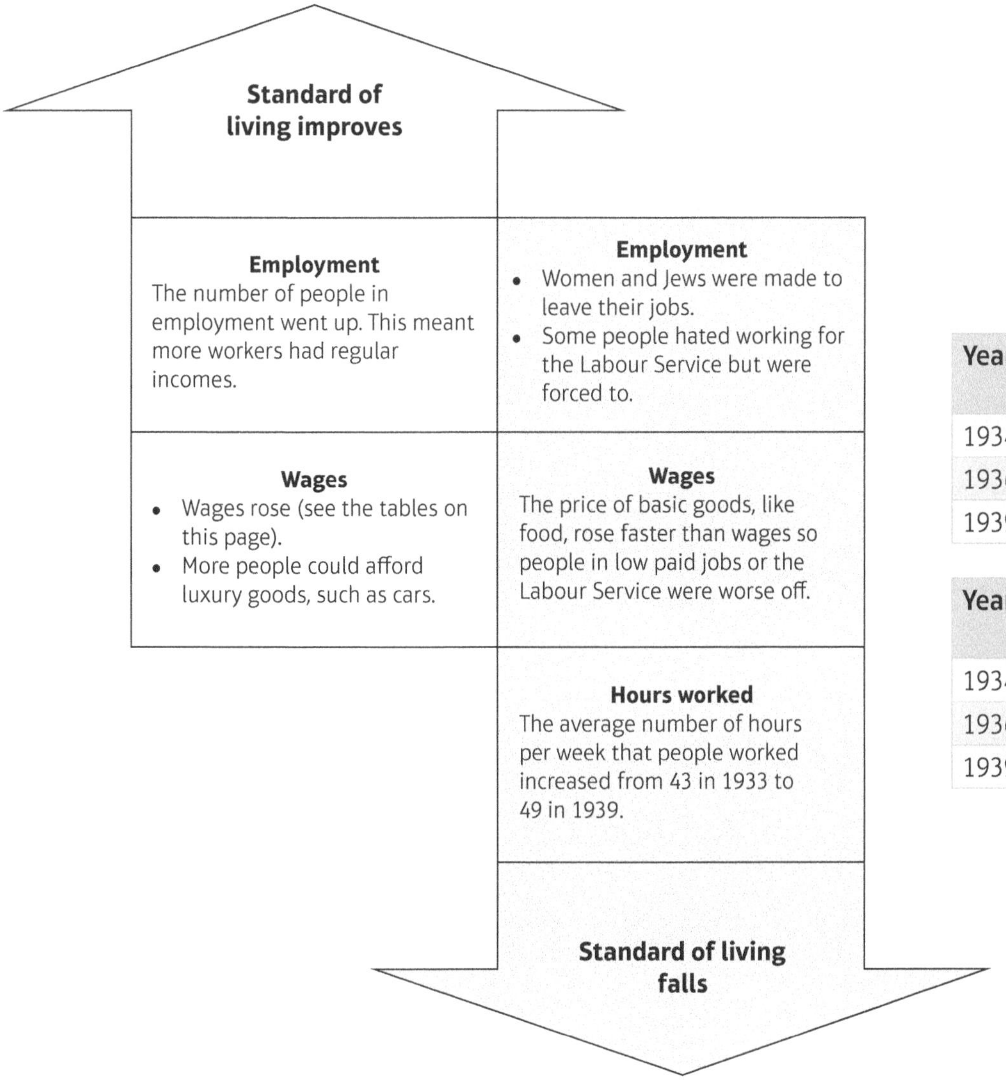
Standard of living improves
Employment
The number of people in employment went up. This meant more workers had regular incomes.
Wages
• Wages rose (see the tables on this page).
• More people could afford luxury goods, such as cars.
Employment
• Women and Jews were made to leave their jobs.
• Some people hated working for the Labour Service but were forced to.
Wages
The price of basic goods, like food, rose faster than wages so people in low paid jobs or the Labour Service were worse off.
Hours worked
The average number of hours per week that people worked increased from 43 in 1933 to 49 in 1939.
Standard of living falls

Year	Rise in wages compared with 1933
1934	6%
1936	9%
1939	20%

Year	Rise in sale of goods compared with 1933
1934	14%
1936	25%
1939	45%

Figure: The standard of living in Nazi Germany, 1939.

Nazi organisations which affected the standard of living of workers

Hitler knew that he must make sure that the economy was strong because this would be good for German workers. If German workers were not happy, the Nazis could start losing support. The Nazis set up a number of organisations to help improve the lives of German workers. The three main ones were: **The Labour Front (DAF)**, **Strength Through Joy (KdF)** and **The Beauty of Labour (SdA)**.

The Labour Front (DAF)

In 1933, the Nazi government banned trade unions. Trade unions work to improve the standard of living of workers, so this was bad for living standards.

In place of trade unions, Hitler set up the DAF (*Deutsche Arbeitsfront*, or German Labour Front) in 1933.

Benefits
- It set out the rights that all workers were entitled to.
- It set a maximum number of hours that could be worked per week, to ensure workers were not overworked.
- It set a minimum wage to ensure that workers were not paid too little.

The German Labour Front (DAF)

Limitations
- Workers were not allowed to negotiate over pay or conditions.
- The number of working hours was quite high – higher than it had been before the 1930s.
- If workers tried to slow down production, for example by going on strike, they would be punished.

Figure: The benefits and limitations of the DAF.

Strength through Joy (KdF)

The Nazis set up another organisation in 1933 to improve the standard of living of workers. Strength through Joy (*Kraft durch Freude*, or KdF) was a part of the DAF.

The purpose of the KdF was to make the benefits of work more enjoyable, so that Germans would see their work as a way to a happy life.

- The KdF provided leisure activities for workers, such as sport events and outings.
- Workers could win holidays.
- The activities were well supported (see Source D).
- Workers were expected to join.
- By 1936, there were 35 million members.

Source D

Official Nazi figures for a selection of Strength through Joy (KdF) activities in the Berlin area, 1933–39.

Type of event	No. of events	No. of people involved
Lectures	19,000	1,000,000
Theatre performances	21,000	11,000,000
Museum tours	60,000	2,500,000
Sports events	400	1,500,000
Hikes	6,000	125,000
Holidays and cruises	1,000	700,000

Source E

A KdF poster, from 1939. It urged workers to give 'just 5 marks a week to drive your own car'.

Beauty of Labour (SdA)

The Beauty of Labour – *Schönheit der Arbeit* or SdA – was set up to provide better facilities for workers, like better toilets and canteens.

- By 1938, the Nazi Party said that nearly 34,000 companies had improved their facilities.
- However, the workers had to do the building and decorating themselves, at no extra pay.

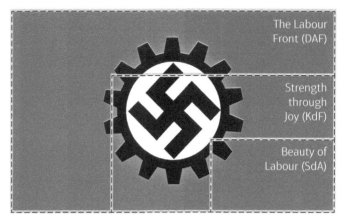

Figure 4.7 The Beauty of Labour was a division of Strength through Joy. Strength through Joy was a division of the Labour Front.

Overall judgement on the standard of living in Nazi Germany

As so many aspects of workers' lives were changing in Nazi Germany, it is difficult to make an overall judgement about whether living standards improved or not. For example, the standard of living may have improved for some people and not others, depending on their circumstances. Interpretations 1 and 2 discuss the real and alleged benefits for German people under the Nazis.

Interpretation 1

From *Life in Germany*, by Steve Waugh, published in 2009.

From 1936 to 1939 wages increased, but this was due to a longer working day rather than an increase in hourly wage rates. In addition, the cost of living rose in the 1930's, which meant that real wages (how much workers could buy) actually fell. There were also food shortages, because the government reduced agricultural production to keep up prices [to help farmers].

Interpretation 2

From *Nationalism, dictatorship and democracy in 20th Century Europe*, by Hall, Shuter, Brown and Williams, published in 2015.

For Germans who conformed to Nazi expectations, living standards went up. Unemployment dropped. Nazi statistics show that real wages rose... though only if a worker worked overtime*. The 'Strength Through Joy' programme provided many extras. Some (benefits), such as loans [and] medical care... were real enough.

Key term

Overtime*

Extra hours that are worked for extra pay.

Exam-style question, Section B

Suggest **one** reason why Interpretations 1 and 2 (pages 129 and 130) give different views about the standard of living of German workers in Nazi Germany.

You may use Sources A and D (pages 123 and 128) to help explain your answer. **4 marks**

Exam tip

A good answer will analyse both interpretations and explain a possible reason why they give different impressions of the quality of life of German workers under the Nazis.

You should try to strengthen your explanation using the sources or information of your own.

Interpretations vary for many reasons, for example because they are based on different sources, give only partial pictures of the situation or differ in which factors they believe are most important.

Summary

- Reducing unemployment was a key aim for Hitler, for political and economic reasons.
- The Nazis used a variety of methods to reduce unemployment. These included the National Labour Service, the building of the autobahn and rearmament.
- As well as official unemployment levels, Nazi Germany also had 'invisible unemployment', where they hid the real numbers of people who were unemployed.
- There were many changes to the standard of living of workers in Nazi Germany. These included changes to unemployment, wages and prices.
- The Labour Front, including Strength through Joy and the Beauty of Labour, also affected the standard of living of German workers.

Checkpoint

Strengthen

S1 What happened to unemployment in Nazi Germany?
S2 In what ways did the Nazis try to reduce unemployment?
S3 Describe changes in wages, prices and the sale of luxury goods in Nazi Germany.
S4 What was the impact on the standard of living of German workers of the Labour Front, Strength through Joy and the Beauty of Labour?

Challenge

C1 Make a judgement about whether the standard of living of workers rose or fell in Nazi Germany.

How confident do you feel about your answers to these questions? If you are unsure, look again at pages 124–126 for S1–S2 and pages 127–129 for S3–S4. For C1, discuss with other people in class. Your teacher can provide hints.

Nazi racial beliefs and policies

The Nazis believed that, to make the German state strong, the German **population** needed to be strong. This belief affected their policy towards minorities* in the population.

Key terms

Eugenics*

The idea that the human race can be improved by controlling who breeds with who.

Minorities*

Groups of people who represent only a small proportion of the total population of a place.

Racial hygiene*

The idea that races should be kept 'pure' by preventing marriage between people of different races.

Source A

A photograph of eugenics being taught in the early 1940s. The chart on the left shows the 'inheritance of musical talent'. The chart on right shows that certain diseases can be inherited.

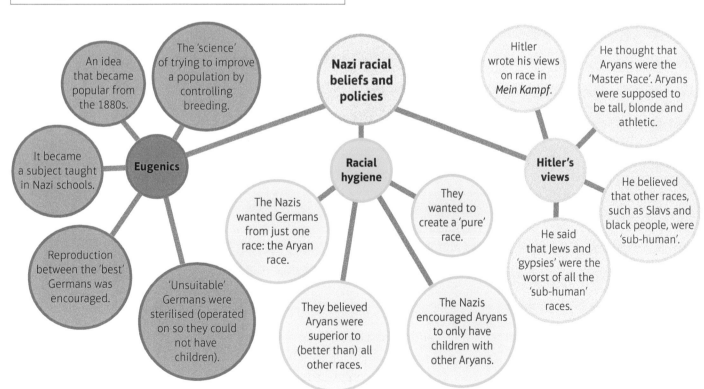

Figure: The Nazis' racial beliefs and policies were based on eugenics, racial hygiene and Hitler's views.

Anti-Semitism

Nazi ideas about eugenics and racial hygiene were particularly aimed against Jews.

Anti-Semitism (hatred of Jews) had been common in Europe for many centuries, for many reasons:

- Most people in Europe were Christian so the Jewish religion, customs and looks made them stand out as 'different'. People can be suspicious of those who are different from themselves.
- Some Christians hated Jews, as they blamed them for the execution of Jesus Christ.
- Some Jews were very successful in business, creating jealousy towards them.

By the 1930s, anti-Semitism had become particularly strong in Germany. There were several reasons:

- When times are hard, people often look for people to blame. Germany had many problems between 1919 and 1933 and some politicians blamed these problems on Jews (even though Jews had not caused the problems).
- Hitler hated Jews (see Source D on page 134) and blamed them for all of Germany's problems.
- Some Germans were influenced by Nazi propaganda (see Source B) and ignored – or even took part in – Nazi persecution* of Jews.

Source B

A Nazi poster, from 1937. The writing says 'The eternal Jew'. The poster was used to turn people against Jews.

Key term

Persecution*

To treat a group of people very badly, for example, due to their religion, race or political views.

Activities

1. **The 15 Second Challenge!** In pairs, try to speak for 15 seconds – without pausing or repeating yourself – on each of the following: a) eugenics, b) racial hygiene, c) Hitler's ideas on race, d) anti-Semitism. Afterwards, write a short paragraph on each to record what you know about them.

2. Source B shows Jews as different from 'normal' Germans – ugly, sinister, cruel, money-grabbing supporters of communism. Can you find the aspects of the poster that suggest these characteristics?

3. Nazi racial beliefs led to the persecution of minorities during the 1930s. To help you record the events of this persecution, make a horizontal timeline showing the years 1933 to 1939.

   a. Above the line, record the events showing the persecution of minority groups on pages 133–134.

   b. Below the line, record the events showing the persecution of Jews on pages 134–137.

The treatment of minorities

Name of minority group: Slavs

Who are they?

The Slavs were from Eastern Europe. By the 1930s many people of Slavic origin lived in Germany.

How were they treated by the Nazis?

- Nazi propaganda and school lessons told Germans that the Slavs were sub-humans.
- The Nazis threatened to invade Slav countries in Eastern Europe for *Lebensraum* – extra living space – for Germany's people.
- Before the Second World War, Slavs were persecuted less than some other minorities.

Name of minority group: 'Gypsies'

Who are they?

'Gypsies' is a name used for the Roma people. They usually travelled from place to place. There were about 26,000 'gypsies' in Germany in the early 1930s.

How were they treated by the Nazis?

- The Nazis believed that 'gypsies' were lazy and didn't pay enough taxes.
- After 1933, 'gypsies' were often arrested and sent to concentration camps.
- From 1936, some 'gypsies' were forced by the Nazis to live in special camps where the living conditions were poor.
- In 1938, 'gypsies' were banned from travelling in groups. They lost German citizenship and social benefits.
- In 1939, orders were given to prepare all 'gypsies' for deportation. This meant that they would be removed from Germany.

Name of minority group: Homosexuals

Who are they?

People who are attracted to people of their own sex.

How were they treated by the Nazis?

- The Nazis believed that homosexuals spoiled the 'purity' of the German race.
- In 1934, 766 men were imprisoned for homosexuality. In 1936, this number was over 4,000. In 1938, it was 8,000.
- Homosexual prisoners were often sent to concentration camps.
- 5,000 German homosexuals died in concentration camps.

People with disabilities

The Nazis believed that people with disabilities were a burden on society (see Source C).

- In 1933, the Nazis made it compulsory for people to be sterilised* if they were disabled.
- 400,000 people were sterilised by 1939.
- In 1939, the Nazis ordered that babies with severe disabilities should be killed. Later, children up to 17 years old with disabilities were also killed.
- Over 5,000 children with disabilities were killed.

Source C

A Nazi poster from 1938. It says '60,000 Reichmarks. This is what the person suffering from hereditary defects (inherited disabilities) costs the Community of Germans during his lifetime. Fellow Citizen, that is your money too.'

The persecution of Jews

In 1933 Jews made up less than 1% of the population of Germany. But before Hitler became Chancellor in 1933, he had made clear that action against Jews would be an important aim for the Nazis.

Source D

Hitler, speaking to an acquaintance, Josef Hell, in 1922.

If I am ever in power, the destruction of the Jews will be my first and most important job. I shall have gallows* after gallows erected in Munich. Then the Jews will be hanged one after another, and they will stay hanging till they stink... Exactly the same procedure will be followed in other cities until Germany is cleansed* of the last Jew.

Persecution begins (1933)

Nazi propaganda called Jews 'vermin' and 'filth' and described them as evil.

The Nazis introduced rules to exclude (keep out) Jews from many parts of German society. For example:

April 1933	Jews banned from government jobs. Jewish teachers sacked.
September 1933	Jews banned from inheriting land.
1934	Some councils banned Jews from parks and swimming pools.
May 1935	Jews banned from the army.

Key terms

Sterilised*

Given surgery to prevent them having children.

Gallows*

The structure on which people are hanged to kill them.

Cleansed*

To get rid of something.

The boycott of Jewish shops and businesses (1933)

This early persecution of Jews included a Nazi campaign against Jewish shops and businesses.

In April 1933, an official boycott* began of all Jewish businesses, doctors and lawyers. SA stormtroopers were sent to paint Jewish stars on shops owned by Jews. They then stood outside with banners to discourage people from going inside.

Source E

A photograph of the boycotting of Jewish shops in 1933. The Nazi sign says *Germans, defend yourselves. Don't buy from Jews*.

The Nuremberg Laws (1935)

Over time, persecution became worse. In 1935, a set of changes called the Nuremberg Laws were passed.

NEWS

The Nuremberg Laws

- Only those of German blood are German citizens.
- Jews are subjects*, not citizens.
- Jews have no right to vote.
- Jews cannot have a German passport.
- Jews cannot marry German citizens.
- Sexual relations between Jews and German citizens are banned.

Der Führer

A. Hitler

Figure: The Nazis passed the Nuremberg Laws to increase the persecution of Jews.

Source F

A photograph from 1933 of a Jewish man, on the right, being accused of having a German girlfriend. They have both been forced by SA and SS members to walk the streets with signs admitting their 'crime'.

From 1938, life in Nazi Germany became even more threatening for Jews:

- March 1938 – Jews had to register all of their possessions, making it easier for the government to take them.
- July 1938 – Jews had to carry identity cards, making it easier for them to be persecuted.

Key terms

Boycott*

When you stop using or doing something, as a protest or punishment.

Subject*

A person who is below someone else in power and importance

Kristallnacht (9–10 November 1938)

Kristallnacht or the Night of Broken Glass took place on 9–10 November 1938 throughout Germany.

The causes of Kristallnacht

- In November 1938, a Jewish man called Herschel Grynszpan went into the German embassy in Paris and shot a German. Grynszpan was angry about the way the Nazis had treated his parents.
- Goebbels, the Nazi Minister for Propaganda, used the event to stir up hatred of Jews in Germany.
- He ordered newspapers to print anti-Jewish articles.
- He got the SA, SS and Gestapo to attack local synagogues* and houses of Jews.

Hitler gets involved

- Goebbels and Hitler decided to turn the violence against Jews into a nationwide attack.
- Nazi leaders were encouraged to arrange attacks on Jews but were told to do so secretly. Police were told not to stop any violence against Jews by members of the public.
- The SS was ordered to arrest as many Jews as the prisons could take.

The violence on 9–10 November

- On 9 and 10 November, gangs smashed and burned Jewish property and attacked Jews.
- Some gangs wore Nazi uniforms. Others were SA and Hitler Youth wearing normal clothes.
- Some Germans were shocked; others watched with pleasure or joined in.
- Official figures listed 814 shops, 171 homes and 191 synagogues destroyed.
- About 100 Jews were killed.

The aftermath

- Goebbels blamed the Jews for starting the trouble and punished them.
- Jews were fined 1 billion marks to pay for the damage.
- By 12 November, 20,000 Jews had been sent to concentration camps.

Source G

A British newspaper, the *Daily Telegraph*, reporting on 12 November 1938.

Mob law ruled in Berlin... as hordes of hooligans went on an orgy of destruction. I have never seen an anti-Jewish outbreak as sickening... fashionably dressed women clapped their hands screaming with glee [and] held up their children to see the 'fun'. No attempt was made by the police to stop the rioters.

Interpretation 1

From *The Third Reich in Power*, by Richard J. Evans, published in 2006.

The violence [during *Kristallnacht*] was familiar from the behaviour of the brownshirts in 1933. But this time it went much further. It was clearly more widespread and more destructive. It demonstrated the hatred of the Jews now gripped not only the stormtroopers and [Nazi] party activists but was spreading to other parts of the population – above all to the young, upon whom five years of Nazism in schools and the Hitler Youth had clearly had an effect.

Interpretation 2

From *Life in Germany*, by Steve Waugh, published in 2009.

This led to Kristallnacht, so called because of the thousands of Jewish shop windows which were smashed... Many Germans watched the events with alarm and concern. However, the Nazi-controlled press presented it as a reaction of ordinary Germans against Jews. Most Germans did not believe this, but hardly anyone protested for fear of arrest and death.

Key term

Synagogues*
Jewish religious buildings.

Activities ?

1. Look at the timeline you produced in response to Activity 3 on page 132. Explain why 1933, 1935 and 1938 are key dates in the Nazi persecution of Jews. Write a sentence for each.

2. As a whole class, discuss why there was so little opposition to the persecution of Jews from members of the public in Nazi Germany. Afterwards, write a paragraph to outline your own views.

The climax of peacetime persecution

In January 1939, the Nazis decided to evict* all Jews from Germany. In April 1939, the Nazi Party ordered that all Jews should be evicted from their homes and collected together for deportation*. This was how things stood when the Second World War broke out in September 1939.

The role of the German people

Most of what happened to Jews between 1933 and 1939 was known, both within Germany and in other countries. Indeed, many Germans took part in the persecution and many others – and most other countries – did little to stop it. This is difficult to understand.

Why didn't more German people oppose how Jews were being treated?

- Some Germans were too scared of being punished if they opposed Nazi ideas and policies.
- Other Germans might have believed that the situation was not that bad, or simply ignored it as it did not affect them.
- Many Germans were taken in by the propaganda and ideas of the time, and felt that the persecution of the Jews was fair.

Extend your knowledge

The bigger picture

The persecution of minorities was worse during the Second World War, which started in 1939. As German troops defeated countries all over Europe, more Jews fell under the control of the Nazis. By the end of the Second World War, it is estimated that the Nazis had murdered 200,000 'gypsies' and six million Jews in concentration camps.

Exam-style question, Section B

How far do you agree with Interpretation 1 about the events of *Kristallnacht* in 1938?

Explain your answer, using Interpretations 1 and 2 (page 136) and your own knowledge of the historical context. **16 marks**

Exam tip

Good answers will create an argument, setting out:

- how far you agree with Interpretation 1, with evidence to support your view. For example, can you give details of how the Nazis made hatred of Jews 'widespread' in Germany?
- how far you disagree with Interpretation 1, again with evidence to support your view. Do you think this event was mostly caused by the general public hating Jews, or was it led by others?

Evidence should come from Interpretation 1 or 2 and your own knowledge.

Key terms

Evict*
Force out.

Deportation*
To be removed from a country.

THINKING HISTORICALLY Cause and Consequence (6a)

Seeing things differently

Different times and places have different sets of ideas. Beliefs about how the world works or how societies should be governed can all be very different from our own. It is important for the historian to take into account these different attitudes when examining people's actions in the past.

Nazi persecution of Jews

During the years 1933–39, the German government officially called Jews vermin and they ruined their businesses, robbed them of German citizenship, banned them from most jobs, destroyed their property, imprisoned them and violently assaulted them.

1 Imagine that the current government of Britain treated Jews like that today. What would be the reaction of the press and the general public?

2 Attitudes in Nazi Germany towards Jews were different from current attitudes in Britain.

   a Write one sentence explaining the attitude of the Nazis towards Jews in the 1930s. Write one sentence explaining the attitude of the British public towards Jews today.

   b Write one sentence explaining the attitudes in German society towards the persecution of Jews in the 1930s. Write one sentence explaining the attitudes in British society towards the persecution of Jews today.

3 Write a paragraph explaining how attitudes in Germany towards Jews in the 1930s contributed to the persecution of Jews under the Nazis.

Summary

- Treatment of minority groups was shaped by eugenics, racial hygiene and anti-Semitism.
- Slavs, 'gypsies', homosexuals and people with disabilities were all mistreated.
- Nazi persecution of Jews began in 1933, became worse in 1935, with the Nuremberg Laws, and then became worse still from 1938 after *Kristallnacht*.

Checkpoint

Strengthen

S1 Describe Nazi beliefs about eugenics, racial hygiene and anti-Semitism.

S2 In what ways did the Nazis mistreat minority groups in Germany?

S3 Describe mistreatment of Jews in 1933, the Nuremberg Laws and *Kristallnacht*.

Challenge

C1 Explain Nazi reasoning behind their persecution of minority groups and Jews.

How confident do you feel about your answers to these questions? If you are unsure, look again at pages 131–132 for S1, pages 133–134 for S2 and pages 134–137 for S3. For C1, discuss with other people in class. Your teacher can provide hints.

Recap: Life in Nazi Germany, 1933–39

Recap quiz

1 What laws did the Nazis introduce to encourage marriage, motherhood and childbirth?
2 What were the main Nazi youth groups for young German girls and boys?
3 What does KdF stand for?
4 What is 'invisible' unemployment?
5 Name the Nazi organisations which affected the standard of living of workers.
6 When did the Nazi boycott of Jewish shops begin?
7 When were the Nuremberg Laws passed?
8 What was forbidden by the Nuremberg Laws?
9 What event caused the beginning of *Kristallnacht*?
10 How many Jews were arrested and taken to concentration camps following *Kristallnacht*?

Activities

1 Match up the following lists:

a	Eugenics is	i	anti-Jewish views
b	Racial hygiene is	ii	the study of selective breeding
c	Hitler believed Aryans were	iii	the worst sub-human race
d	Slavs were thought to be	iv	the master race
e	Jews were thought to be	v	choosing parents for racial purity
f	Anti-Semitism means	vii	sub-humans

2 Decide whether each of these statements is true or false.

   a Slavs were from Eastern Europe.
   b Slav people, such as the Poles, occupied land that Hitler wanted for German *Lebensraum*.
   c 'Gypsies' was the name the Nazis used for the Roma people.
   d There were two million 'gypsies' in Germany in 1933.
   e 'Gypsies' were often sent to concentration camps.
   f From 1936 some 'gypsies' were made to live in special camps.
   g 5,000 homosexuals died in Nazi concentration camps.
   h Nazi laws banned marriage between Jews and non-Jews.
   i In 1933, the Nazis made it compulsory for disabled people to be sterilised.
   j From 1939, the Nazis had a policy of killing disabled children.

3 Give three reasons why few Germans might have objected to the persecution of Jews.

Explaining why historians' interpretations differ

In Paper 3, one question will ask you to suggest one reason why two interpretations give different views about an aspect of your study. To understand the reasons for difference you need to know that:

- historians choose different things to focus on
- they make judgements about the topics they study
- they might use different sources of evidence.

Historians focus on different things

Historians construct interpretations based on evidence from the past. Think of their role as similar to a house-builder: the sources of evidence available are the building blocks for their construction. Historians choose what questions to ask of the materials available to them.

No historian can write about the whole of history everywhere. What shapes the historian's work is what they want to explore and what they choose to focus on. Figure 1 below lists some of the choices they make:

Place	National history	Local history
Period	One century or more	One decade or less
Range	Overview	Depth
People	National leaders	Ordinary people
Aspect	Political history (looking at changes in governments and politics)	Social history (looking at changes in attitudes and customs)

Figure 1 Some examples of historians' choices.

Figure 2 The historian's focus.

Historians A and B below are both writing about the same school, but their focus is different. In looking at the history of a school, several different enquiries are possible, for example the focus could be on the building, the curriculum, students' achievements and so on. As you read the interpretations below, identify what the two historians are interested in – what have their enquiries focused on?

Historian A

The village school has been in continuous use since 1870. It continues to educate local children from the ages of 5 to 11. They are educated in the same building that was constructed in 1870. Its outward appearance has hardly changed. It was originally built of red brick, with white-painted wooden doors and the large windows that can still be seen today. The schoolroom windows, reaching almost to the high celling, were designed to give plenty of light, but with windowsills too high for students to be distracted by being able to see anything outside. Although a modern extension at the rear was added in the 1960s, the key features of the school building represent a remarkable degree of continuity in education in the locality.

Historian B

Education locally has changed in the period since 1870. Lessons in the 19th century focused almost entirely on the 3Rs of reading, writing and arithmetic. There was much learning by heart and copying out of passages. By the 21st century, the wall displays and the students' exercise books show that science, history, geography, have all become important parts of the curriculum and with more emphasis on finding out and creativity. In terms of the curriculum, the degree of change in education since 1870 has been considerable.

Historians reach different conclusions from the evidence

Even when historians have the same focus and purpose – for example, even if they both aim to explain why the same thing happened – their conclusions may still be different. This is because the evidence from the past doesn't give us an answer: historians have to work out an answer from it – and often the evidence points in different directions. Then, the historians have to make judgements. Differences may arise because:

- they have given weight to different sources: considering some sources to be more important or more useful than others
- they have reached different conclusions on the same sources.

Summary

- What shapes the historian's work is the aspect of history the historian chooses to explore.
- Historians' judgements differ because the evidence can support different views. They may reach different conclusions because they have given weight to different sources.

141

Preparing for your GCSE Paper 3 exam

Paper 3 overview

Your Paper 3 is in two sections that examine the Modern Depth Study. In Section A, you answer one question on a source and one using your own knowledge. Section B is a case study using sources and interpretations of history, and the four questions will be about the same issue. The paper is worth 30% of your History assessment.

History Paper 3	Modern Depth Study		Time 1 hour 20 minutes
Section A	Answer 2 questions	16 marks	20 minutes
Section B	Answer 4 questions	32 marks + 4 for SPaG	60 minutes

Modern Depth Option 31 Weimar and Nazi Germany 1918–39

Section A

You will answer Questions 1 and 2.

1 Give two things you can infer from Source A about... (4 marks)

Source A is on the question paper. You should work out two inferences from it. An inference is something not directly stated in the source, but which you can work out using details from it.

You have different sections to complete for each inference: 'What I can infer. . .' and 'Details in the source that tell me this'. Allow five minutes to read the source and to write your answer. This question is only worth four marks, so you should keep the answer brief and not try to put more information on extra lines.

2 Explain why... (12 marks)

This question asks you to explain the reasons why something happened. Allow 15 minutes to write your answer. You are given two information points as prompts to help you. You do not have to use the prompts and you will not lose marks by leaving them

out. You can add in new points of your own as well, if you can think of any. Aim to write an answer giving at least three explained reasons.

Section B

You will answer Questions 3 (a), (b), (c) and (d). All four questions will be about the same issue. Question (a) will be based on contemporary sources (evidence from the period you are studying). Questions (b), (c) and (d) will be based on two historical interpretations.

3(a) How useful are Sources A and B for an enquiry into... (8 marks)

You are given two sources to evaluate. They are in a separate sources booklet so you can keep them in front of you while you write your answer. Allow 15 minutes for this question to give yourself time to read both sources carefully. Make sure your answer uses both sources and use your knowledge when you evaluate each source. For example, you could use your knowledge to say whether you think the source is accurate, or whether you think it has missed out anything important.

You should make a judgement about the usefulness of each source, saying whether or not you think that the source is, overall, useful or not. You should always take account of the provenance (the nature, origin and purpose) of the source when you think about the usefulness of the information it gives. How reliable is it?

3(b) Study Interpretations 1 and 2. They give different views about...

What is the main difference between these views? (4 marks)

Allow ten minutes for this question to give yourself time to read the extracts. Identify an overall difference rather than different pieces of information. For example, think about whether one is positive and the other negative. Then use details from both interpretations. 'The difference is... this is shown because Interpretation 1 says…, …, but Interpretation 2 says…'.

3(c) Suggest one reason why Interpretations 1 and 2 give different views about... (4 marks)

Allow five minutes for this question. It does not need a long answer but you will need to use both extracts again. Give a clear reason for the difference. One reason could be because the historians have chosen to give weight to different evidence. If you use this reason, you should use both Sources B and C to show that the evidence from the period is different to what it says in the interpretations. If you use other reasons, for example about what the historian is focusing on, you will not need to use Sources B and C.

3(d) How far do you agree with Interpretation [1 or 2] about...? (16 marks + 4 marks SPaG)

This question, including SPaG, is worth 20 marks – over one-third of your marks for the whole of the Modern Depth Study. Make sure you have kept 30 minutes of the exam time to answer it and to check your spelling, punctuation and grammar. Question (d) asks you how far you agree with the view in one of the interpretations (1 or 2). Plan your answer before you begin to write, putting your points in two columns: For and Against. You should use points from the two interpretations and also use your own contextual

knowledge. Think about it as if you were putting weight on each side to decide what your judgement is going to be for the conclusion.

In this question, four extra marks will be gained for good spelling, punctuation and grammar (SPaG). Try also to use relevant specialist terms – for example, terms such as constitution, communism, legislation.

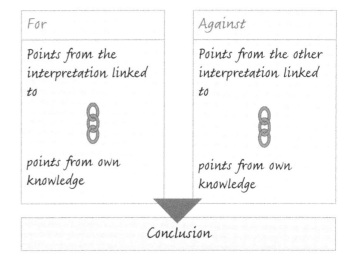

Paper 3, Section A: Question 1

Study Source A on page 100.
Give **two** things you can infer from Source A about how Hitler kept power.
Complete the table below to explain your answer. **(4 marks)**

Exam tip

Make two inferences and choose details from the source that directly support them. The examples below give only the first inference and support.

Basic answer

What I can infer:
Germany had suffered many severe problems, which Hitler helped to solve.

Details in the source that tell me this:
The Treaty of Versailles was unfair and unemployment went up in the Depression.

The inference is correct, but the detail given to support it is not from the source.

Verdict

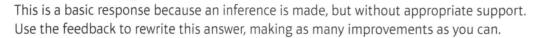

This is a basic response because an inference is made, but without appropriate support.
Use the feedback to rewrite this answer, making as many improvements as you can.

Good answer

What I can infer:
Germany had suffered many severe problems, which Hitler helped to solve.

Details in the source that tell me this:
Source says that Hitler 'saved his country from utter despondency and degradation'.

Details are given that support a correct inference.

Verdict

This is a good response because an inference is made and supported by the source.

Paper 3, Section A: Question 2

Explain why unemployment fell in Germany between 1933 and 1939. You may use the following in your answer:

- National Labour Service (RAD)
- autobahns.

You **must** also use information of your own. **(12 marks)**

Exam tip

Focus on explaining 'why'. Aim to give at least three clear reasons.

Basic answer

The National Labour Service (RAD) paid people for doing public works, like planting trees and draining marshes. Workers wore uniforms, lived in camps and did military drills and parades as well as working.

Work on autobahns also made unemployment fall. This was when roads were built.

Overall, new jobs explain why unemployment fell in Germany.

The factor provided in the question (the RAD) is used. Accurate detail about the RAD is given, but there is no attempt to relate this factor to the question (how the RAD reduced unemployment).

Answer covers the second factor in the question, but it gives very little detail.

Also, no own factors are covered in the answer (only the two factors given in the question).

Conclusion attempts to address the question directly, but it does not explain how new jobs were created.

Verdict

This is a basic answer because:

- it includes a little detailed knowledge
- there is limited explanation of how these factors (the RAD and the autobahns) led to a decline in Germany's unemployment
- no factors from own knowledge are included.

Use the feedback to rewrite this answer, making as many improvements as you can.

Paper 3, Section A: Question 2

Explain why unemployment fell in Germany between 1933 and 1939. (**12 marks**)

Good answer

The National Labour Service (RAD) paid people for doing public works, like planting trees and draining marshes.

At first, the RAD was voluntary. But from 1935 it was compulsory. Workers wore uniforms, lived in camps and did military drills and parades as well as working. People working for the RAD were not counted as unemployed.

Work on autobahns also made unemployment fall. From 1933, Hitler ordered the building of large, fast roads across Germany. This work required a lot of men, and created many new jobs in construction. This decreased the number of unemployed people.

Hitler introduced conscription in Germany in 1935. This meant that more people were employed as soldiers. Hitler's armed forces needed armaments and vehicles and uniforms, so this was a boost to Germany's industries, like the arms industry, coal and iron and steel and textiles.

Overall, the creation of new jobs and conscription explain why unemployment fell in Germany.

> One factor provided in the question (the RAD) is used. Accurate detail about the RAD is given. There is a basic link to the question showing how the RAD reduced unemployment.

> Answer includes own factor (conscription) and there is some detailed information given. It also explains how conscription reduced unemployment.

> The conclusion directly answers the question.

Verdict

This is a good answer because:

- it includes detailed knowledge
- three different factors are covered, including one from own knowledge
- the conclusion directly and clearly answers the question.

The answer could be improved further by linking each point more clearly to the fall in unemployment.

Adding some figures to the answer would also help improve it. For example you could say that half a million men were employed by the RAD by the mid-1930s.

Paper 3, Section B: Question 3a

Study Sources C and D on pages 69–70.
How useful are Sources C and D for an enquiry into the way Hitler came to power?
Explain your answer, using Sources C and D and your own knowledge of the historical context.
(8 marks)

Exam tip

Consider the strengths and weaknesses of the evidence. Your evaluation must link to the enquiry (the way Hitler came to power) and use own knowledge. Include points about:

- what information is relevant and what you can infer from the source
- how the provenance (nature, origin, purpose) of each source affects its usefulness.

Basic answer

Source C is useful because it mentions how Brüning kept issuing commands but he was not obeyed.

A relevant section of the source is mentioned but it is not explained why this information is useful. No inference is made.

But Source C is a story, so we can't be sure that it is describing how things really were.

It is good that the answer considers the provenance of the source, but it is only a brief comment.

Source D is useful. It shows that Hitler needed the help of two other people to lift him to power.

A valid inference is made here, but details should be taken from the source to support the inference. Also, the provenance of Source D has not been considered.

Verdict

This is a basic answer because:

- it has used both sources
- it has made an inference from Source D, but has not made any inferences from Source C
- the provenance of the sources needs to be considered further.

Use the feedback to rewrite this answer, making as many improvements as you can.

Paper 3, Section B: Question 3a

How useful are Sources C and D for an enquiry into the way Hitler came to power?
Explain your answer, using Sources C and D and your own knowledge of the historical context. **(8 marks)**

Good answer

Source C is useful because it mentions how Brüning kept issuing commands but he was not obeyed. This shows that the existing government could not solve Germany's problems, so people wanted to turn to somebody else.

> A relevant section of the source is mentioned and the answer tells us how it would be useful for this enquiry. Inferences are made.

Source C is also useful because it shows that Germany was in chaos. Unemployment was at five million by 1932 and this caused street violence like Source C says, so Germany needed a strong hand, like Hitler. But Source C is a story, so we can't be sure that it is describing how things really were.

> The idea that Germany was in chaos and needed a strong hand is valid inference. Some own knowledge about unemployment is used. Provenance of the source is mentioned briefly.

Source D is useful. It shows that Hitler needed the help of two other people to lift him to power. It comes from a British political magazine, so it shows a political point of view from Britain about Hitler coming to power.

> A valid point is made in the last paragraph. It starts to discuss the importance of the provenance, but needs to develop this idea and link it to usefulness.

Verdict

This is a good answer because:

- it has taken relevant information from both sources and used inferences to show how the sources can be useful
- it has used a bit of contextual knowledge
- the provenance of the sources is considered.

The answer could be improved further by linking the provenance of each source more clearly to usefulness. For example, because Source D is a British cartoon, you could say that it shows British views – not the views of people in Germany. This makes it less useful for the enquiry.

Paper 3, Section B: Questions 3b-c

Study Interpretations 1 and 2 on page 153. They give different views about the way Hitler came to power.
What is the main difference between these views?
Explain your answer, using details from both interpretations.
(4 marks)

Exam tip

Remember to identify a main difference and then use details from both interpretations to support your answer.

Basic answer

A main difference is that Interpretation 1 emphasises the view that problems with the economy in Germany was the reason Hitler came to power. Interpretation 2 says that von Papen and Hindenburg were the reason. It says 'Von Papen convinced President Hindenburg that a coalition with Hitler would save Germany'.

A valid difference is identified but no details are given from Interpretation 1.

Verdict

This is a basic answer because it identifies a difference, with some detail from Interpretation 2, but it does not use detail from Interpretation 1 to support the difference.
Use the feedback to rewrite this answer, making as many improvements as you can.

Suggest **one** reason why Interpretations 1 and 2 give different views about how Hitler came to power.
You may use Sources C and D on pages 69–70 to help explain your answer. **(4 marks)**

Exam tip

Give a clear reason. If you decide to use Sources C and D, choose details from them to show that the historians may have given weight to different sources.

Basic answer

The interpretations may differ because the historians have focused on different issues. Interpretation 1 emphasises the political weakness of Brüning and the Reichstag in explaining why the Nazis became the biggest party.

A reason is given as to why the interpretations may differ, but nothing is said about Interpretation 2.

Verdict

This is a basic answer because it gives a valid reason for the different views. However, it does not use both interpretations to support this reason.

Use the feedback to rewrite this answer, making as many improvements as you can.

Paper 3, Section B: Questions 3b–c

Study Interpretations 1 and 2. They give different views about how Hitler came to power.
What is the main difference between these views?
Explain your answer, using details from both interpretations. **(4 marks)**

Good answer

A main difference is that Interpretation 1 emphasises the view that the social and political chaos in Germany was the reason Hitler came to power. It says that businesses collapsed and unemployment went up and that democracy was replaced by dictatorship and that, as a result, more people showed an interest in Hitler.

On the other hand, Interpretation 2 says that von Papen and Hindenburg were the reason. It says 'von Papen convinced President Hindenburg that a coalition with Hitler would save Germany'.

Details from both Interpretation 1 and Interpretation 2 explain the main difference between the two views.

Verdict

This is a good answer because it identifies a valid difference with support from both interpretations.

Suggest **one** reason why Interpretations 1 and 2 give different views about Hitler's rise to power.
You may use Sources C and D on pages 69–70 to help explain your answer. **(4 marks)**

Good answer

The interpretations may differ because the historians have given weight to different sources. For example, Source C describes the political weakness of Brüning and the social unrest in Germany and says that was why Hitler became more popular. That supports Interpretation 1, which emphasises the political weakness of Brüning and the Reichstag in explaining why the Nazis became the biggest party.

The author of Interpretation 2 has given more weight to sources like Source D about the actions of politicians.

A reason for the difference between the interpretations is given, and Source C is used to support the answer about Interpretation 1.

Interpretation 2 is mentioned and linked to Source D, but the answer would be better if this explanation was more developed.

Verdict

This is a good answer because it gives a valid reason for the different views and supports it using a source. It could be improved further by exploring the other interpretation more.

Paper 3, Section B: Question 3d

Up to 4 marks of the total for this question will be awarded for spelling, punctuation, grammar and use of specialist terminology.

How far do you agree with Interpretation 1 about the way Hitler came to power?

Explain your answer, using both interpretations and your knowledge of the historical context. **(20 marks)**

Exam tip

Be clear what view the interpretation gives and then consider points for and against this view from both interpretations and your own knowledge. Make a judgement, giving reasons for your decision.

Basic answer

Interpretation 1 says that there was a depression in Germany and that this caused problems. It also says that the politicians couldn't solve these problems so people showed interest in Hitler's ideas and voted for Nazi representatives. This is true because when things were bad in Germany, people did start to support the Nazis more.

The answer starts well by explaining the view in Interpretation 1, but the student hasn't added much evidence from their own knowledge to support the view.

Interpretation 2 explains how von Papen convinced Hindenburg to make Hitler Chancellor. This isn't mentioned by Interpretation 1.

Relevant details are chosen to contrast Interpretation 1 with Interpretation 2 but no own knowledge is added in. Also, a judgement is not given.

Verdict

This is a basic answer because:

- it includes relevant details from both the interpretations and a little bit of own knowledge
- it does not give enough detail
- spelling is accurate but opportunities are missed to use key terms. For example, it could have referred to 'the Depression' rather than saying 'when things were bad in Germany'.

Use the feedback to rewrite this answer, making as many improvements as you can.

Paper 3, Section B: Question 3d

How far do you agree with Interpretation 1 about the way Hitler came to power?
Explain your answer, using both interpretations and your knowledge of the historical context. **(20 marks)**

Good answer

Interpretation 1 says that there was a Depression in Germany and that this caused problems. It also says that the politicians couldn't solve these problems so people showed interest in Hitler's ideas and voted for Nazi representatives. From my own knowledge I know that unemployment went up to five million in 1932 and that Hitler got 13 million votes in the presidential election. This shows that Interpretation 1 is correct when it says that the Depression led to support for the Nazis.

Relevant details from Interpretation 1 are used and the student's own knowledge is included. This knowledge is used to clearly support the view of the interpretation.

But Interpretation 1 does not explain how Hitler became Chancellor. It says people supported Hitler and the Nazis but there were no elections for the Chancellor so the people could not choose him. The Chancellor had to be chosen by President Hindenburg. Interpretation 2 explains how Hindenburg decided to choose Hitler as Chancellor.

Relevant details are chosen to contrast Interpretation 1 with Interpretation 2 and own knowledge is added in.

Overall, I agree with the view in Interpretation 1, but it doesn't give all of the reasons why Hitler came to power.

A judgement is given, but this is not fully explained with details.

Verdict

This is a good answer because:

- both interpretations are discussed using detailed own knowledge
- it keeps focus on the question and a clear judgement is given
- SPaG demonstrates accuracy, and uses some specialist terms.

The answer could be improved further by adding in more evidence from your own knowledge that supports or doesn't support the view in Interpretation 1.

The judgement could also be explained more fully.

Interpretations Booklet

Interpretation 1

From *Weimar and Nazi Germany*, by Stephen Lee (1996).

… between 1929 and 1933 crisis returned in full force. Germany experienced a serious depression. This caused the collapse of businesses and an increase in unemployment. The moderate parties of the Weimar Republic could not agree… More use was made of Article 48. The Reichstag was by-passed. Democracy was replaced by dictatorship. A larger part of the population showed interest in Hitler's ideas. The result was that the Nazis became the biggest party in the Reichstag. [They] gave Hitler power, hoping he would use it as they wanted.

Interpretation 2

From *Nazi Germany 1930–39*, by Steve Waugh and John Wright (2007).

Von Papen was determined to regain power. He met Hitler and agreed that Hitler would lead a government with von Papen as the Vice-Chancellor. Intrigue took the place of open political debate. The landowners and leaders of industry were convinced that von Papen and Hitler were saving Germany from Schleicher's military take-over. Von Papen convinced President Hindenburg that a coalition with Hitler would save Germany. Von Papen said that he could control Hitler. On 30 January, Adolf Hitler became Chancellor of Germany.

Answers to Germany Recap Questions

Chapter 1

1 Friedrich Ebert
2 SPD
3 Paul von Hindenburg
4 Gustav Stresemann
5 1929
6 Reichsrat
7 21
8 Chancellor
9 This part of the constitution said that, in a crisis, the chancellor could ask the president to pass a necessary law, by decree, without the support of the Reichstag
10 KPD, SPD, DDP, ZP, DVP, DNVP, NSDAP

Chapter 2

1 German Workers' Party
2 National Socialist German Workers' Party
3 A Nazi newspaper
4 Hitler's own personal bodyguard
5 A violent uprising intended to overthrow existing leaders
6 Paul von Hindenburg
7 Heinrich Bruning
8 Franz von Papen
9 Kurt von Schleicher
10 Adolf Hitler

Chapter 3

1 27 February 1933
2 23 March 1933
3 30 June 1934
4 Heinrich Himmler
5 Reinhard Heydrich
6 Joseph Goebbels
7 A way of controlling art and culture so it was consistent with Nazi ideas
8 Martin Niemöller
9 The Edelweiss Pirates
10 The Swing Youth

Chapter 4

1 The Law for the Encouragement of Marriage, 1933, and divorce laws to encourage childbirth.
2 Little Fellows, German Young People, Hitler Youth; Young Maidens, League of German Maidens.
3 Strength Through Joy
4 The Nazis found ways to reduce the number of people recorded as unemployed. The real number of unemployed people was higher than the official figures.
5 The Labour Front (DAF)Blood
6 1933
7 1936
8 The Reich Law for the Protection of German Blood and Honour20,000
9 Herschel Grynszpan's murder of Ernst vom Rath
10 20,000

Index

Note: Page numbers followed by *f* represent figures.

Acknowledgements
Picture credits

The publisher would like to thank the following for their kind permission to reproduce their photographs.

(Key: b-bottom; c-centre; l-left; r-right; t-top)

COVER : Bridgeman Images: Private Collection

Alamy Stock Photo: Chronicle 7t, 11, 76, Hi-Story 8, 17, Granger Historical Picture Archive 13, interfoto/History 19, 74, 95, Fine Art Images/Heritage Image Partnership Ltd 37l, Trinity Mirror/ Mirrorpix 94, CBW 134, Bridgeman Images: German School, (20th century) / Kunstgewerbe Museum, Zurich, Switzerland/Archives Charmet 21, Garvens, Oskar Theodor (1874–1951)/Bibliotheque Nationale, Paris, France/Archives Charmet 29, Dix, Otto (1891–1969) / Staatsgalerie, Stuttgart, Germany 37r, German School, (20th century) / Private Collection / Peter Newark Military Pictures 42, 56, Schmitt, H. (fl.1940)/Private Collection/Peter Newark Pictures 51,Schilling, E. (fl.1923)/Bibliotheque Nationale, Paris, France/Archives Charmet 52, German School, (20th century)/Private Collection/Peter Newark Military Pictures 68, German School, (20th century)/Private Collection/Peter Newark Pictures 88, German Photographer, (20th century)/Private Collection/Look and Learn/Elgar Collection 91, Wissel, Adolf (1894–1973)/Deutsches Historisches Museum, Berlin, Germany 109,Hoffmann, Heinrich (1885–1957)/Private Collection/The Stapleton Collection 114, German School, (20th century) / Private Collection / Archives Charmet 129,**BPK (Bildarchiv Preussischer Kulturbesitz):** 28, 30, Kunstbibliothek, SMB/Dietmar Katz 35, 75, 112. **DACS: Olaf Gulbransson 30, Dix, Otto (1891–1969) 37r. Daily Express:** BCA 78. **Getty Images: New York Times Co/Archive Photos 7b, 135l, Bettmann 14, 23, 124, World History Archive 24, Ullstein bild Dtl. 44, 81, 96, Keystone/ Stringer/Hulton Archive 50, 97, 116, Imagno/Hulton Archive 59, Hulton Archive/Stringer 64, Roger Viollet Collection 89, Universal History Archive/Universal Images Group 102, 132, Herbert Hoffmann/, Ullstein bild Dtl 111, Heinrich Hoffmann/Ullstein bild Dtl 123, Keystone / Staff/ Hulton Archive 135r. Mary Evans Picture Library:** Mary Evans/ Sueddeutsche Zeitung Photo 108, 117, 120, 131**. Punch Limited:** 70. **Super Stock:** Past Pix/Science and Society 46. **Topfoto:** Ullsteinbild 55, 67, 85.

Text credits

We are grateful to the following for permission to reproduce copyright material.

Taylor and francis: From The Weimar Republic by John Hiden, published in 1996. 9, 45, 63, **Saxon House:** Rosa Leviné-Meyer,Leviné: the life of a revolutionary,Saxon House, 1973. 15, **Anton Pannekoek:** The German Revolution - First Stage,Anton Pannekoek 1918. 15, **Penguin Random House**: From The Coming of the Third Reich by Richard J. Evans, published in 2004. 15, 19, 49, 54, 62. From The Nazis: A Warning from History, by Laurence Rees, published in 2005. 85, Detlev Peukert, Inside Nazi Germany: Conformity, Opposition and Racism in Everyday Life, Penguin, 1993. 121, From The Third Reich in Power, by Richard J. Evans, published in 2006. 136, John Tolund," From Adolf Hitler", published in 1996. 51, 64, From *Berlin Stories*, by Christopher Isherwood, published in 1945. 69, **Hachette UK**: From Nazism and War by Richard Bessel, published in 2013. 20, **Charles G. Dawes**: The Dawes Plan, 1924. 27, **Owen D. Young**: The Young Plan, 1929. 28, **Gustav Stresemann**: An extract from Stresemann's speech on Germany's entry into the League of Nations, 1926. 30, **Macmillan**: From Knaves, Fools and Heroes by Sir John W heeler-Bennet, published in 1974. 77, **Social Democratic Party**: From an official report by the SPD(Social Democratic Party) about theraid on their Braunschweig branch in March 1933. 77, **Butterworth**: From the book Hitler Speaks, published in 1940, by Hermann Rauschning, a Nazi official who emigrated from Germany in 1936. Here, he is quoting words spoken by Ernst Röhm, when he was drunk in 1934. 79, **Alfred Rosenberg**: Extracts from the diary of Alfred Rosenberg from 30 June 1934. Rosenberg was a leading Nazi. 79, **Pearson Education Limited**: From Life in Germany 1919–1945, by Steve Waugh, published in 2009. 80, 129, 136, Edexcel GCSE History A: The Making of the Modern World Unit 2A: Germany 1918-39 John Child Pearson 2013 Daily Telegraph, November 1938. 136, From Weimar and Nazi Germany, by Stephen Lee (1996). 153, **Adolf Hitler**: A speech by Hitler in the Reichstag, on 13 July 1934. 80, Extracts from a speech by Hitler in the Reichstag on the Enabling Law, March 1933. 88, Hitler, addressing a Nazi rally in Nuremberg in 1934. 109, An extract from a speech by Adolf Hitler in 1933. 116, 119, From a speech by Hitler to his ministers in February 1933. 124, Hitler, speaking to an acquaintance, Josef Hell, in 1922. 134, A. Hitler, The Nuremburg Laws. 135, "An extract from a speech made by Adolf Hitler at the Bergerbrau Keller on the evening of 8 November 1923" 53, "From a letter, written by Hitler in 1924, while in prison after the Munich Putsch" 54, Hitler's speech to the people of Germany on the day of his appointment as Chancellor of Germany on 31 January 1933. 64, **Heinrich Himmler**: Himmler addressing the Committee for Police Law in 1936. 84, Himmler, speaking to SS commanders, 18 February 1937. 84, **Hans Frank**: A speech by Hans Frank from 1936. Hitler appointed Frank as President of the German Academy of Law. 87, **Nazi publishing house**: Hitler writing in M Kampf (Hitler's autobiography) in 1925. 91, "Mein Kampf by Adolf Hitler" 55, **Joseph Goebbels**: Steve Waugh, WJEC Eduqas GCSE History: Germany in transition, 1919–39. 91, A statement by Joseph Goebbels in April 1933. 94, Joseph Goebbels, a leading Nazi, describing the role of women in 1929. 109, **Nazi Propaganda**: Ministry of Propaganda order, 1935. 92, **United States Holocaust Memorial Museum :** From the website of the US Holocaust Memorial Museum, opened in 1993 to record details of the treatment of the Jews by Nazi Germany. 95, **Hodder and Stoughton**: Germany: The Third Reich. 100, **Bloomsbury Publishing**: From The Nazi Dictatorship, by Ian Kershaw, published in 1985. 100, Martin Niemöller: Part of a lesson used frequently by Martin Niemöller in sermons and speeches. He used it to condemn Church leaders who did little to speak out against the evils of

Nazi Germany in the 1930s. 101, **University of Exeter Press**: Jeremy Noakes, Geoffrey Pridham, Nazism, 1919–1945: The German home front in World War II, University of Exeter Press, 1998. 103, **Randall Bytwerk**: A speech by Gertrud Scholtz-Klink, Reich Women's Leader, in 1936. 110, **Traudl Junge**: Traudl Junge was a young woman in Nazi Germany. Here she is remembering her youth in Nazi Germany. 112, **Caliban Books**: Henry Metelmann, A Hitler Youth: Growing Up in Germany in the 1930s. 118, **Cambridge University Press**: An extract from Modern Germany, by V. R. Berghahn (1982). 118, **United States Government Printing Office**: Source of English translation: Law for the Reestablishment of the Professional Civil Service (April 7, 1933). In United States Chief Counsel for the Prosecution of Axis Criminality, Nazi Conspiracy and Aggression, Volume III. Washington, DC: United States Government Printing Office, 1946. 121, **Kraft durch Freude**: Official Nazi figures for a selection of Strength through Joy (KdF) activities in the Berlin area, 1933–39. 128, **Hachette UK**: From Nationalism, dictatorship and democracy in 20th Century Europe, by Hall, Shuter, Brown and Williams, published in 2015. 130, **NSDAP:** From the Twenty-Five Point Programme, originally produced by the DAP in February 1920. 43, A confidential report on the Nazis by the Interior Ministry, July 1927. 58, **Nazi party**: "A quotation from a supporter at a Nazi Party meeting",1926. 44, From an interview with a member of the Nazi Party. 62, **Gerhard Rempel**: "From an article by Gerhard Rempel on Hitler's style of Leadership" 46, **Bavarian state police**: "From a report in September 1923 by the Bavarian police" 49, **Gustav von Kahr:** Gustav von Kahr," An announcement made on 9 November 1923", leader of the state government of Bavaria. 50, **New Directions Publishing**: From Berlin Stories, by Christopher Isherwood, published in 1945, 69.